LAST WRITES

LAST WRITES

WILLIAM WATSON

William H Watson was born in the smokey suburbs of Pittsburgh, Pennsylvania during WW II, too young to grasp its significance but old enough to be shaped by the impact of a family without a father at home. That would continue long after the war was over. He was the first person in anyone's knowledge, other than his school teachers, to earn a college degree. Pouring over the section on electricity in an old encyclopedia, he decided early to become an electrical engineer. After graduation, he shot like an arrow through his working years to arrive at retirement laden with fears that the next generation would not repeat his experience. That fear and the impact of finding himself in his seventies and growing old have influenced his writing. Still searching for some essential truths to guide his remaining journey, he has assembled the essays presented here

Copyright © 2023 by WILLIAM WATSON

All rights reserved. No part of this book may be reproduced in any manner whatsoever without written permission except in the case of brief quotations embodied in critical articles and reviews.

First Printing, 2023

DEDICATION

This book is dedicated to my niece, Claire Watson, who died of mucolipidosis II two years ago. It's a genetic disorder commonly referred to as "I-cell" disease. It's rare and, unfortunately, untreatable. Their lifespan is short, but Claire lived a long fourteen years. We grieved, cried, and celebrated the many beautiful gifts she gave us. . Our lives were forever changed. Sometimes in grief, we can find moments of steadfast love and joy, which was the case for me. She changed me forever, so I am grateful and dedicate this book to her memory.

I miss you, Claire. Please read my essay for her on page 34.

CONTENTS

DEDICATION   v

1	INTRODUCTION	1
2	COLLECTION: GOD AND RELIGION	3
3	DO YOU BELIEVE IN GOD OR SOMETHING ELSE?	4
4	GOD AND SANTA CLAUS	6
5	GOD AND THE SOUL	11
6	WHERE DOES GOD HANG OUT?	14
7	THERE IS A GOD, AND HE IS DIGITAL	15
8	GOD IS A REPUBLICAN	17
9	GOD, MAN, AND TOMATOES	18
10	GOD NEEDS TIME OFF	20
11	COLLECTION: THE JOURNEY	22
12	IF OLD BICYCLES COULD TALK	23
13	BIRTHDAY RESIGNATION - IT'S YOUR TURN NOW	26
14	GROWING OLD IN A CATTLE FEEDLOT	28

15	CHILDHOOD INVENTORY	31
16	GOODBYE TO SELF	33
17	FINDING HAPPINESS LATE IN LIFE	35
18	LIFE DESCRIBED IN 75 WORDS	39
19	A LIFE HALF LIVED	41
20	THE MAN BEFORE YOU	43
21	TIME TO MOVE ON	44
22	PERMISSION TO SPEAK FREELY, SIR?	47
23	I RESIGN; IT'S YOUR TURN	53
24	LEARNING ABOUT SEX IN A SUPERMARKET CHECKOUT LINE	56
25	STUCK IN SECOND GEAR	59
26	SUPERMAN AND WONDER WOMAN CAN'T HELP YOU	62
27	PERSPECTIVE IS WORTH 10 IQ POINTS	65
28	THANKS FOR THE HEART ATTACK	67
29	THE SILENT GENERATION	72
30	TRUMAN SHOW IN MY RETIREMENT COMMUNITY	77
31	WHEELS ON MY SHOES, GROWING UP IN A SMALL TOWN	80
32	COLLECTION: LOVE AND LOVING	87
33	CAT LOVE	88
34	CLAIRE'S WORLD	89
35	ONE FINAL WORD ABOUT LOVE	91

36	HAROLD ALBERT WATSON	94
37	HOW I SURVIVE	96
38	A LOVE LETTER TO EMMA WATSON	98
39	NEVER LOVED A PEACH?	100
40	DO I LOVE OR HATE MY BODY?	101
41	MY MOTHER, THE VAMP	104
42	COLLECTION: TRANSCENDENCE	105
43	FLYING HIGH	106
44	GREEN CURRY AND RICE	108
45	FINDING TRANSCENDENCE AT 30K FEET	110
46	COLLECTION: ECONOMICS	112
47	BRADDOCK	113
48	JOBS AIN'T COMING BACK	115
49	LAST ENGINEER STANDING	118
50	PITTSBURGH	121
51	THE RICH NEED YOUR HELP	123
52	URBAN GLEANER	126
53	THERE ARE WHITE BUSSES IN HEAVEN	128
54	COLLECTION: DEATH AND DYING	130
55	THE ARC OF A MAN'S LIFE — THE LONELY JOURNEY FROM WOMB TO TOMB	131
56	RUNNING OUT OF TIME: MY CHINESE CLOCK SAYS SO	135
57	CROSSING THE LINE	137

58	FALLING	138
59	GROWING OLD WITH MIRRORS	140
60	LAST CURTAIN CALL	143
61	LETTERS FROM HOSPICE	145
62	LOGAN'S RUN FOR SENIORS	148
63	MUSICAL CHAIRS	150
64	ON DEATH AND DYING	153
65	THE WAY THE WORLD ENDS	156
66	COLLECTION: WAR	157
67	D DAY	158
68	TENTH ANNIVERSARY OF THE IRAQ WAR	160
69	MEMORIAL DAY 2022	162
70	STICK ENVY	164
71	TOO OLD FOR THE NEXT WAR	166
72	VETERANS DAY 2018	168
73	VETERANS DAY 2019	170
74	COLLECTION: POLITICS	172
75	PRESIDENT TRUMPKE	173
76	REPUBLICAN NICENE CREED	175
77	FLORIDA SANTA LEGISLATION	177
78	COLLECTION: EVERYTHING ELSE	178
79	THE BEST WAY TO TELL	179
80	CONFESSIONS OF A SEVENTY-SOMETHING BICYCLIST	181

81	BODY LOVE HATE	184
82	DIGNITY	187
83	DAMN YOU, MARK ZUCKERBERG	188
84	GERALDINE IS OVERWEIGHT AND BLACK	191
85	SHOULD I GOOGLE OR WIKIE?	195
86	SEVENTY YEARS OF ROLLER SKATING	197
87	MY CAT LOVER	199
88	I MAY BE TOO BUSY VOLUNTEERING TO RIDE NEXT YEAR'S CENTURY	200
89	ODE TO BETSY	203
90	SEVEN REASON WHY OPRA DOESN'T RETURN YOUR CALLS	204
91	HOW TO PUBLISH A GREAT NOVEL	207
92	YOUR FRIENDLY SUPERMARKET	210
93	TOOLS	213
94	YOU DON'T OWN YOUR CAT	218
95	ZEN AND THE LOVE OF BICYCLE RIDING	220
96	SHORT STORY: ABBY'S BABY	223
97	BOOK EXCERPT: "MADE IN AMERICA" CHAPTER ONE	235

CHAPTER 1

INTRODUCTION

Turning sixty-five offered the promise of retirement and endless periods to re-discover my inner soul, take long bicycle rides, reflect on my accomplishments and failures, and time with friends and family with no sense of urgency to job or other obligations. It made large openings in my life to explore new ideas and activities.

Well past eighty, the next door opens to my mortality and the short period before death. It is the last wicket in a croquet game, not quite over, but definitely on the wain. The reminders are everywhere: friends suffering from the diseases of aging, complaints of restless legs, arthritis joint pain, and a loss of energy and enthusiasm for life. And the funerals.

Somewhere in my life's arc, I can no longer say I am still young, middle-aged, senior, or even "young at heart." It wouldn't take much, maybe a subtle hunch in the shoulders, a hesitation to answer a simple question, a struggle for the right word, or a watering of the eyes to pass into the realm of the elderly, or maybe less forgiving comments like "old man."

It's our universal fast, and there's comfort in that, but it doesn't mean I have to accept my passing life without some reflection or effort to make sense of it. The meaning of life still eludes our best thinkers, suggesting that it is something very personal and not a universal truth.

And so, this collection of essays is my musing about what I know about life and what I think about dying. Don't look in these lines for your truth; you'll have to find your way to the other side. From what I have learned so far and late in life, the path is about your family and the people in your immediate world. These people call me Bill and smile when they see me.

CHAPTER 2

COLLECTION: GOD AND RELIGION

CHAPTER 3

DO YOU BELIEVE IN GOD OR SOMETHING ELSE?

Do you believe in God, that He fashioned the earth in seven days and rested on the seventh?

Do you believe in the coded messages in the bible, their interpretation hinging on the translated English word for covet, abomination, sin, and hundreds of other words that risk your salvation?

Have you transcended traditional religions to a plane of your design, a blend of eastern and western religions, Christianity and Judaism, and elements of Buddhism and Confucianism? This salty brew sits nicely on your palette.

Did your "higher power" create the universe, like some master craftsman in a shipyard who then kicked the staves and let the boat float away, a ship of fools left to chart their destiny? Or is your God at the tiller, guiding our path and showing us the way?

Does the idea of a godless existence strike fear in your heart? Can you believe that we are born and die with no greater purpose than to fulfill a biological imperative?

Is your path the one true path, and are you one of God's chosen people? How do you feel about those who are not with you?

Have you reconciled the cruel and devastating impact of war and natural disaster as part of God's plan or something of nature and man's doing?

When a baby dies, does your God ignore the crib side petitions for a purpose beyond our understanding?

Have you thought about forces and energy that defy our ability to scale or understand their magnitude: the mass of the earth, the total radiated power of the sun in any given instant, the gravitational forces that bind our galaxy and the universe?

Did you know that the first atomic bomb, called "Little Boy," was dropped over Hiroshima on August 6, 1945, and killed 140,000 Japanese people using no more than two pounds of uranium 235?

Did you know that a quart of cow's milk weighs just over two pounds?

Can you construct a bridge between religion and science that places a supreme being in command of the infinite energy of the universe at the same time as one who witnesses the creation or death of a single cell?

Can you help me across that bridge?

CHAPTER 4

GOD AND SANTA CLAUS

IS THERE A GOD?

Since god is ephemeral, there is no way to prove or disprove His existence with certainty. For billions of people, God does exist. His presence is fashioned by the influence of their peers, parents, and persons of religious authority who tap into the human need to be loved, watched over, and seen. And the existence of God explains how the universe was created and how our time on earth has an exit ramp to heaven and an everlasting communion with God. It takes away the terrible fear that we die. We are not like animals; we have a soul that lives eternally with God.

So why is there not a single religion? A religion that unites the world with the same shared belief. The answer to that question is complex and has historical roots. Early man created a god or gods to explain the many unknowns in his life. God caused the sun to rise ... and set. And he is being tribal; these pockets of "religion" vary across the globe. The passage of time and the gradual unification of peoples came too late and too uneven to provide a single pathway to one God.

The organization and institutionalism of religion provided the final blow to any universal belief system. It became a means to create a nation or state and give it a uniqueness that would exclude others and create sharp boundaries. Differences, rather than similarities, feeds the human need to be uniquely defined.

There is no doubt that religion and belief in God satisfy a human need. Furthermore, there is no doubt that the fulfillment of this need has had many unintended consequences. Consequences that have shaped our history, for better or worse, since man's existence.

Organized religions, like the Catholic Church, have a large bureaucracy and a highly structured management framework. It has vast financial requirements, including properties and investments worldwide. Those burdens require creating and maintaining a large following that will fuel these costs. To do so, formalism and doctrine must be carefully cultivated to meet the needs of the parishioners and keep them in the pews. In the early days, people were uneducated and gullible. The Domestic sword of eternal salvation was put in place and quickly managed to keep the institution viable.

Over the centuries, however, the molding of faith through religious dogma has become more complex. The doctrine of faith is now riddled with conflicting ideas about God, interpretations of His will, and ways to live a life of faith. Is He merciful, loving, vengeful, all-knowing, omnipresent, forgiving, or one of many attributes that fit our human needs or other attributes created to keep the believer on a narrow path?

Over the centuries, the province of God has narrowed as science, astronomy, and more sophisticated human reasoning have displaced God's role. It has created a conflict in His definition and a problem for religions. Believers in today's world must set aside their common sense and reasoning and put belief in God into a special place in their minds that cannot be challenged. God's presence in our lives has become more personal and molded to our needs. There have been too many instances of Him being cruel, with floods and hurricanes, lacking compassion for oppressed people, and ignoring our petitions for intervention to save our lives from disease and cruelty. God can't be counted on to solve our significant problems, but He can be at your side for comfort and support in your everyday life.

In the final analysis, a believer in God, especially one who belongs to an organized religion, must set aside the politics and pettiness of religious institutions. Ignore the inherent contradiction in the doctrine of faith, and accept that God is capricious and sometimes absent, even in our most needy time. And if we find that hard to get, we are told it's because, as humans, we cannot know the mind of God. Turning away from Him means turning away from his comfort and your salvation. Not a choice.

IS THERE A SANTA CLAUS?

As children, we are introduced to two belief systems (ignoring the Easter Bunny) that have surprising similarities. Both require faith in a father-like figure that resides in a faraway place.

One that knows what you are doing and can see into your life. Belief in Santa precedes faith in God in some aspects. If you are evil, for example, Santa will take note of it and leave you no toys. If you don't believe in him, there will be no toys. No reward.

God is an invention of the human mind to comprehend and accept what we do not know, especially the reality of death as the end of our existence. God and religion promise another life, maybe an even better one. It gives meaning to our lives. And it makes it easier to hand over our trust in God and then go about daily living.

The church (organized religion) does not allow me to come to that conclusion, claiming that the human mind is incapable of understanding the mystery of God and His ways. The burden of proving there is no God falls heavily on me; proving there is a God is something rarely asked of anyone.

My rational mind rebels at that prohibition from the perspective that if there is a God, and He created heaven and earth and gave me a mind that could fathom such existence (or not), then it is within my province to declare Him honest or not by the reasoning power He gave me. It's a convoluted argument that hangs on a slender thread.

Although nothing can be proven, one way or the other, there is sufficient evidence to make it evident and irrefutable. Or is there?

In all recorded history, the goal line of what is known vs. The unknown has moved from God toward accepting rational and scientific thought. Early God-man, the sun rose and set, or so it seemed. Until astronomy took that chore from Him. And slowly, at first, then as an avalanche, our understanding of science has stripped God of credit for what is attributable to the large body of deterministic science.

And now, in the echoing halls of cathedrals, God has retreated to the last vestiges of why we are here and why the universe behaves as it does, the ultimate mystery that still defies an answer.

Evolution, if accepted, can explain life's pathway, and science can roll back the clock to the instant of all creation. But there is always enough wiggle room for God to have laid His hand in that blinding flash of creation. But it begs the question: did He then "walk" away? Some think that; it explains much of human behavior we have difficulty accepting as Christian or moral. And it explains the vagaries of nature and medicine that have their way with us.

For obvious reasons, organized religion has co-opted all that is good from early times. A war that is won. A child's life that was saved from disease. A storm that moves away from a crowded city. These are prayers answered... or so it seems. However, explaining all the unanswered prayers moves the conversation to the mirky area of not understanding God's will. Or His way.

Could a loving, compassionate God take a child from a crib so it could be with Him in heaven? Could thousands die from a tsunami because our prayers were not strong enough, or worse because He took that opportunity to punish us for some imagined sin, like homosexuality?

We need God's comfort that we accept these unknowns, locking them in a part of our brain for things we don't understand, and then constructing a happy life with a loving God watching over us day and day and night and for some, living with the idea that we are born and then die and nothing more is a psychological wound too deep to live with.

Arguments about the existence of God and the benefits of having a strong belief in Him often cite a belief that religion is a positive force. It keeps man and society in harmony by asking believers to follow a moral code God has set forth.

CHAPTER 5

GOD AND THE SOUL

I'm not sure I believe in God. You may wake up every day with a certainty of His existence, but I'm one of those waiting for a sign. Or maybe I'm someone who has to put their hand in the wound, like Thomas. Nevertheless, God or no God, I have no doubts about the existence of the soul; I don't know if it survives death and makes its way to heaven or anywhere else.

My soul is the intangible abstraction of who I am. It has nothing to do with my body but everything with who I am and what I believe. If you draw a stick figure of a person, it has no soul. But if you add a thought bubble and a single word, a soul starts to form. For that reason, a baby develops a soul moments after birth and continues that process for the rest of its life.

The most exciting question about souls is how much and when we choose to reveal and share them with others. A relationship of any substance is one where the soul door is wide open; on the other hand, a shallow relationship gives us only the tiniest glimpse of another's soul. Our lives are filled with both, but we long for and celebrate the former. A soulmate is two souls with a large conduit of sharing and honesty connecting them. The rewards are great, but not without a price. When you reveal your soul to someone, you are highly vulnerable to being judged or mocked. That's why we live to meter and protect our souls' exposure. It makes sense—we don't want to be hurt—yet it's the reason we may live a short and lonely life.

Library shelves are sagging with the number of books written to help us navigate the world of relationships. The word "soul" may never be mentioned, but it's at the heart of the matter. There is the personal aspect of cultivating and nurturing your soul and then choosing to reveal it to others. Both parts are important and deserve our attention. Still, it is the revealing side that "carries the freight" and moves us entirely into love, family, friends, country, and, for some, a relationship with a higher being.

If you are willing to take risks, soul-sharing will lead to a rich life filled with people and relationships that bloom, flourish, and are filled with joy. Everyone who has taken this path will tell you it's worth the occasional pain and hardship. The negative side of it can become the foil that will lead to an increased sense of beauty and wonder. Only you can make a choice. Only you can open the door.

Now that you have a soul connection with someone, wouldn't it be nice if it could last forever? Enter religion. It says, yes, our soul will live forever in heaven (or some religions would have a "bad" soul quickly winging its way to a fiery hell). We can "live" forever in an afterlife with God in heaven, a place that has been given various descriptions that suggest both something physical (seated on the right hand of God and "seeing" out friends and family), as well as spiritual, were, for example, we will have everlasting happiness and freedom from want.

We may go to heaven to be with friends and family, but for most religions, the privilege of eternal life is not extended to animals. Was that God's plan, or does it reveal arrogance on our part? Would the idea of animals—God's creation—being in heaven with us somehow diminish the afterlife in any way? Many, like myself, feel their pet has a soul that rises above a simple definition of animal behavior. I'm a cat lover; dog lovers would be more vociferous about the existence of a dog soul and their close bond with it. In a pathetic attempt to make the best of the religious prohibition, we have invented the concept of "doggie heaven" or "cat heaven," etc., for non-human animals.

Most religions, including the Christian faith, have long regarded the animal world as created by God but utterly subject to human domination and use, like the minerals and oil in the ground. We have been given dominion over the earth with no rules or consequences. Animals with souls would be a great inconvenience, especially in the large industry of raising animals for meat consumption. No clergy has picketed a slaughterhouse or appealed to the pulpit for being humane to animals. Contrast that attitude with the American Indian, who killed animals only to eat and use their pelts to stay warm, and always with respect for their spirit. Yet we called them "savages" and did our best to remove them from the planet.

Ultimately, you may take your cue from religion and set hard lines or decide whether you or an animal has a soul. As you move through your life, the decision may not be as difficult as you think. The soul sitting, standing, or even wagging its tail next to you may be all that matters.

CHAPTER 6

WHERE DOES GOD HANG OUT?

I imagine He is at the trail-end of science, sitting there, explaining the mirky terror that comes from our lack of understanding of what lies ahead. An early man witnessed the sun rising and thanked Him for another day. He took credit for what astronomers struggled to understand... and later did, over time, much to the consternation of the church. God moved up the trail as we now ponder the mysteries of DNA and black matter at the universe's edge (if there is one). He is there to offer a faith that He created all you don't understand, the part that science cannot explain. Maybe the trail ends at the big bang. God was there and was the creator of what has become our galactic journey. His work done, could religion be the fabrication of man to help us live with the uncertainty of a slowly moving trail-end? Has religion done more harm than good? Count the bodies of lives lost in the name of religion. Witness the holy men (and politicians) willingly marching us to climatological destruction—something to think about.

CHAPTER 7

THERE IS A GOD, AND HE IS DIGITAL

The debate over the existence of an "analog" God will forever continue. The evidence of His presence is physical. The Bible, Tora, grand cathedrals, monuments, statues, and several tons of wood from the cross that crucified Jesus. Wood, ink, and stone all proclaim His legitimacy. Institutions across the globe collect our donations of money and mind to perpetuate His hold for the top spot in our spiritual and cosmic biosphere ... until now.

What did we miss?

In true binary fashion, the universe went from nothing to existence so quickly that we can label our origin as binary. These facts point to the presence of a digital God. The most elemental constituents of the universe are binary pieces of the physical world. All the analog fragments of life are made from binary components. Just like music from a streaming source is analog (we hear it), all the details that makeup how it got to our ears are digital until the end of this digital "food chain."

Our God is the digital-to-analog conversion of digital pieces scattered across the universe. Like a digital photo, God takes a physical form in this reconstruction so that our mind can assemble Him to please our longing for something we can see.

This new digital religion is not new. Gottfried Leibniz, 1689, invented the binary system. His discovery prompted the early beginning of followers who embraced a digital viewpoint. Over time, and with accelerating speed, we have been putting in place the concepts and means to bring our digital God into every aspect of our being.

We connect with God over WiFi; he is with us every moment of our day, switching to cellular data when we stray from local networks. We can speak to Him and ask for his intervention in our lives by asking Alexa or Google for His help.

The high priests of this religion are not holy men with fertile imaginations but engineers and scientists whose rationality and the quest for digital perfection (no lost bits) make them a new kind of clergy. Programmers create works akin to the gospels and biblical tomes of our past. Small pieces of His being are embedded in toasters, coffee makers, and nearly all aspects of our world. The analog God is put aside as merely a step toward reaching digital perfection.

From time to time, God has inspired men to create fundamental building blocks for his digital world, like the invention of TCP/IP. God speaks to us using the TCP/IP protocol. The complexity of the digital mystery of His voice reaching us speaks to the perfection and majesty of a digital world. No analog God could do that.

The one true God is digital. The passage of time will reinforce that truth. You are likely reading this on an instrument of a digital God's creation.

Rest in Peace / Enter a Wait State with no Interrupts

CHAPTER 8

GOD IS A REPUBLICAN

We believe in one God, a Republican, creator of all things wealthy and successful. We believe in one Political party, Republican, maker of small government and low taxes. We believe in one Republican president, the bible branded and funded by all things rich and influential. Through him and with him, the government will get out of the way, and we will be ruled according to the whims of the religious right. For us and our salvation, the next president will come from Texas and be anointed by the Tea Party* as a true believer. May goodness and large political donations follow him for the rest of his days in power. Amen

CHAPTER 9

GOD, MAN, AND TOMATOES

When we die, we cease to exist in the material world. But the earth, our world, is a closed system, and the material aspects of our past life continue to inhibit the planet, but in a lower, elemental form. We may enclose them in a cement vault, but they are still here.

The idea that we will live on in some spiritual or mystic form and perhaps be untied with our maker and see loved ones is the invention of religion to help us cope with the disappointment of no longer being in existence. It also serves the purpose of imagining a better place where our burdens, disappointments, and failings are lifted from us. My life is terrible, but I will be at peace in heaven.

Religion is a way to unify people with a common belief, and its lack of verification can better sustain its existence. It can passivate groups of people who rely on religion to support them rather than take action and thereby threaten the structure of the oppressors. It can be used as a rationale to kill, despite its tenants against killing. And finally, for the employees of the religious institution, it is a job and a way to imagine a higher calling to service.

The fact that there are multiple religions, sometimes with radically different tenants, is understandable. Religions started on a regional basis, and local individuals with only fragmentary knowledge of historical religions structured the belief system. Creating high walls of belief was a way to unite its followers and defend its existence. And not surprisingly, it can also be used to kill and conquer religious followers with a different faith.

CHAPTER 10

GOD NEEDS TIME OFF

Given the workload associated with the presidential inauguration and various crises worldwide, GOD has made it known through His worldly embassies that He can no longer maintain His omnipresence and provide the necessary blessings and endorsements to meet the obligations of His contract. He cites the unusually high demand for His attention brought on by circumstances that, frankly, go well beyond the sins of Adam and Eve and speak to an "axis of evil" that was not planned for by His Father.

He also notes gross copyright infringements in using His name and logo and the lack of compensation and credit guaranteed by His franchise rights. He cites numerous instances of His name being used to endorse products and causes that He has not approved or adequately vetted. In some cases, outcomes are promised that exceed the scope of His contract, not to mention His heavenly powers.

"All of this abuse has got to stop. I am not a vengeful GOD, but even deities have their limits." He has called for a moratorium on using His name except in global emergencies, pestilence, natural disasters, and large-scale famine. In some cases, for example, a tsunami or volcanic eruption, it should be understood that a conflict of interest exists for

Him, and once initiated, outcomes are beyond His control.

To reduce the burden on God, world leaders are calling for the invocation of other deities on a rotating basis. A global clearinghouse will be created to coordinate these efforts. Representatives will be dispatched to disaster sites to provide on-the-scene brokerage of higher appeals for mercy, forgiveness, or mundane things, like food, shelter, blankets, etc.

May GOD* be with you,

* used with His permission, all rights reserved

CHAPTER 11

COLLECTION: THE JOURNEY

CHAPTER 12

IF OLD BICYCLES COULD TALK

If my late nineteen seventies Nishiki International bike could talk, I'd be in big trouble. She would tell a tale of abuse and neglect, maybe get me arrested. It didn't start that way; it began as a love affair. When I blew out my back from ten years of running on Palo Alto, California streets, I looked for another way to get my chemical fix – those addictive drugs I knew as the "runner's high." With two kids in college and a second mortgage, the back surgeon said it would be OK to start running again. I didn't believe him. A bike seemed like the right thing, and for $500, she was pretty as any bride.

We were inseparable. On weekends we climbed the long grade into the hills above San Francisco and traversed Skyline Drive. We stopped at Alice's restaurant, a place like a song, where "you can get anything you want . . ." We watched the motorcycle riders gather across the street in lines ten and twenty. The riders hung out, argued whose bike was the best, and told tales of missed curves, riders flung off the road into the dense brush and never found for months. Sometimes I ignored the reality of the painful return ride and slipped over the hill and began the miles and miles of downhill to Pescadero Beach to stand on the sandy cliff above the Pacific Ocean . . . with my girl.

We commuted to work at Ampex in Redwood City through a maze of back streets. I felt like an early ecological warrior — smug and self-righteous. Biking was so famous that the city fathers created bike lanes and had them painted on the roadway. Everything seemed so perfect, but then it suddenly ended. There was no farewell ride, no goodbyes on the sand cliff, just an unceremonious last trip to the garage and her placement on two hooks in the ceiling. She looked like a slaughtered animal, gutted and splayed for draining, her vital oils dripping, her grease coagulating. Except for a few rides around the block, it was to remain that way for the next twenty years, surviving move after move, kept but unloved.

It's 2008, and things are looking up for Nishiki-girl, thanks to my good friends John and Lydia. They told me about their bike club, The McHenry County Bike Club, describing the ride schedule and group events in great detail. And they said they were friendly people! The level of the activity expressed suggested that members wore their biking clothes 24 X 7 (I still think that). It was agreed that I would accompany them on a get-acquainted ride.

Not wanting to look like an out-of-shape wimp, I knew I needed some preparation, and I didn't know if my old bike was up to the task. Stephen, the president of Sleepy Hollow and the owner of the Bike Garage in East Dundee, was my savior, giving me good advice and agreeing to keep the "old girl" alive at least until winter. I spent $20 per wheel for new tires and tubes, an outrageous sum compared to the amount paid for the last set. I started a few training rides to travel five miles before I stopped to rest. I gradually expanded my range and, at the same time, got to know the beautiful Fox River Bike trail. When I rode non-stop to St. Charles, albeit a sweating husk of a person when I arrived, I knew I was ready.

My first ride with the club was a re-make of the movie "Easy Rider," with me taking Jack Nicholson's part. At least I had an authentic bicycle helmet, not a football helmet. The rest of my wardrobe consisted of walking shorts, a logo tee shirt from one of my Silicon Valley jobs, and a newly purchased pair of shoes from K-Mart. My new water bottle smelled and tasted like plastic. My bike looked like something Sam would ride.

Over the weeks, I transformed: first a club shirt, then a $20 odometer from Dicks. As an entry model, it doesn't tell me my heart rate, what gear I'm in, or how much elevation I climbed, but I do know when to turn left or right. I then affixed my new GPS to the handlebars and took pride in announcing the road ahead, hundreds of yards before the old-timers. I learned to shout "car back" and to avoid saying "clear" to watch the last rider get whacked by a car. Well, it was clear.

Soon, I was paid a high compliment. "You do all right for only having ten speeds." My takeaway is that if I had 20 or 30 speeds, I would do even better, maybe watch Dianne's image fade to a tiny dot in my rearview mirror. The K-Mart shoes remain, but I have shed the walking shorts for a pair of biking shorts. They rank up there with gunpowder and the transistor as the world's greatest inventions. Suddenly I think a century ride would be possible.

I keep my Nishiki in the back of my car all the time. At first, I said it was there in case of an emergency so that I could ride for help. If I'm honest, I have to admit I want to be with her as much as possible. It's love re-bloomed.

If I ever fall prey to the temptation to look for a new bike, I will gently remove Nishiki from the car and park her on the side of the garage. I don't want her to see me looking at other bikes. I can't be that cruel, not again.

CHAPTER 13

BIRTHDAY RESIGNATION - IT'S YOUR TURN NOW

I resign. Yes, at age 73, I decided to pack it in. No, not on life, but any responsibility I bear for the state of the world. I haven't done an excellent job in my lifetime, and now it's clear that Sisyphus needs to give up. That rock will not budge on what's left of my watch. It's your turn. Shoulder up!

In the lead-up to the Vietnam War, I was assigned to Germany and drank beer, and drove my sports car around Europe. I did my two years, got out, never looked back, never looked at the newsreels of death and carnage, and never joined a peace march. When civil rights demonstrations and protests were held and people were killed in Mississippi, I hid in my work as an engineer. And now, late in life, with employment over, children raised, and finally having eyes wide open to the sad blight of the world, I find my ability to dent the fabric of the universe out of my grasp. Oh, I'll still do small acts of kindness and look for volunteer jobs to give something back, but the heavy lifting that's up to you.

Here are the significant issues (a baker's dozen) that I'm turning over to you:

- **Gay marriage.** Two people who love each other should be able to marry. I'm tired of hearing "bible" arguments about the alleged harm it would do to me. Slavery was a tradition in the south. Enough! Maybe someone will put down their bible and listen to *you*.
- **Rising ocean levels and global warming.** People who think science is not in or that the earth is 6,000 years old annoy me and should be barred from attending bible school. They seem to be good Christians; maybe they want to get to heaven sooner. I live 105 feet above sea level, so I'm okay for my lifetime.
- **Deforestation of the Amazon.** So, third-world people want to clear the land and raise crops to feed their families. We pillaged the ground and killed most Indians here; it's hard for us to be sanctimonious about it. Maybe we should help you (find another way).
- **Animal extinction.** Tinkering with the delicate balance of nature doesn't seem like a good idea. Commercial raising of hogs with hundreds of animals per acre doesn't either. Need Rhino horns to help your sex life? Better solve this one right away.
- **Gridlocked and dysfunctional government.** Can you imagine flying a spaceship and there is only one control? Okay, that is what we have, the vote. I've tried, but I think we're f---ed.
- **I am shrinking middle class.** I've tried my best not to shrink. Unfortunately, the wealthy 1% have more votes and influence than you or I. This has been going on (the decline) for 30 years. Maybe we need more data? More food stamps? More soup kitchens?
- **Global terrorism.** I'm done with the Bush "war on terrorism." I don't know any terrorists, and I don't want to spend any of my precious time left looking for one.
- **Poverty.** Since we have *never* tackled to root cause of poverty, why start now? Even if I gave away all my money, the statistic wouldn't budge. You can choose to ignore it at your own risk. Buy a house in a gated community.

CHAPTER 14

GROWING OLD IN A CATTLE FEEDLOT

How did I get to this cattle feedlot? You look around, and it's a dismal and crowded place. There is plenty to eat, but corn is not your favorite, and you're standing ankle-deep in cow shit.

Yesterday you were eating grass in a sunny field with your friends. Mom and dad died a while back—do you think they did? One day they just disappeared, no real goodbyes, everyone saying they went to a better place.

Time passed. You did well on the ranch. You followed the herd when it made sense and went your way when it didn't. You found grass and stayed well-fed without being the one in the front. Trouble happened; some got hurt, but not you. Maybe you were lucky; perhaps you just had more cow sense?

Calves were born; the herd got larger. After some time, you were older than most, but you could still easily keep up. Nothing could change once you were told it was time for retirement. Retirement? The pronouncement said, "you don't have to work for your grass anymore; you will be taken care of and well-fed." So, you reluctantly boarded the trailer, not having a choice, yet in a way, excited for this next adventure.

Not long after the truck delivered you to the feedlot, the realization sunk in that retirement wouldn't be easy. Was it a lie? Not a single blade of grass anywhere. Nothing in your vision for the rest of your life would ever be green. And the grass was one thing you loved the most. And those aches and pains you ignored in the pasture suddenly started haunting your days. If only you could run, exercise?

It's boring and lonely; you're no longer with your pasture friends. You make an effort anyway. You tell the guy next to you, "tell me about your pasture time." "It was okay," you hear. The conversation goes nowhere. A glazed look comes over him. "I'm hungry, he says, "I think I'll have some more corn."

Is this all there is? You ask yourself. Are you eating, shitting, and getting old? For what?

The "for what" soon becomes apparent. One day there is a stirring in the herd. You can smell the fear in the air. Something is not correct. You are being herded toward a circular ramp. Someone said Temple Grandin built it. Who was Temple Grandin? That question will never be answered; you move slowly to the entrance.

"You're next, " the human shouts. Me? NO! You mooo and tell him you have to tinkle, then break away to find a place to hide. No matter, his attention is on the next one in line. "You're next."

Days before, word had spread that the ramp led to a better place. There would be grass, as much as you like. And you would never get old. You could see your parents, dad, and friends from the pasture. Forever.

You never believed any of it. Not a single word. That ramp led to someone's dinner table. You just knew it.

Trucks arrived, and you mingled with the new "retirees." They seem younger than you. Will there always be trucks, endless trucks? When you got a chance, you told them that you must avoid the ramp at all costs. But they wouldn't listen; they headed immediately for the corn.

The next time at the entrance to the ramp, you mooed that you needed to say goodbye to a friend. And the next time you needed to have a bit of corn before…

It was working! But in truth, you were getting tired. Tired of the same corn diet, tired of the banal conversation, tired of missing your friends. You had one last excuse: you needed to think about it. It was a lame excuse, and it didn't work.

Climbing the circular ramp for the first time, you could see more feed lots—as far as the eye could see— and a parade of trucks approaching. The morning sun is shown in your eyes for the first time in memory. The fear was palpable; ahead, there was reluctance and shaky legs. Not you. You moved ahead. You were mustering your best walking ability. It was time. Your time.

The last few steps came too soon. You moved ahead, thinking about grass, the greenest, freshest grass you have ever known.

CHAPTER 15

CHILDHOOD INVENTORY

Toys Given to me by my Parents:

Lionel construction set
Lincoln logs
Marbles
Gyroscope
Flexible flyer sled
Wooden skis
Archery bow
A machine gun that emitted sparks
Lionel "O" gauge train set (engines, track, villages)
Balloon tire scooter from Holland
B-B gun
Football helmet (blue)

Inherited Toys (hand-me-downs from sisters):

White (girls) ice skates
Girls' bicycle (single-speed, coaster brake)

Toys That I Created:

Spear (a straight length of a tree branch with a carved, pointed end)
"David" sling (a rock in the bottom of an old nylon stocking)
Slingshot (made from a "Y" shaped tree branch
Arrows made from dowels, bird feathers, and metal tips
Firecracker guns are created from metal pipes and ball-bearing "bullets."
Marble incline/ramp made from old curtain rods
Building blocks from wood construction scraps
Crystal radio (no power required) made from wire wrapped on a Quaker Oats container
Rubber band guns made from (natural rubber) auto-inner tubes
Rocks that were the right size and weight for throwing
Shacks made from materials from the city dump

Source of Knowledge / Learning:

School and textbooks
1939 Encyclopedia Britannica
Years of National Geographic
Sears Catalog
A book with a blue cover on sexuality
My town needed a public library.
My friends
Cousins and uncles
Radio Amateurs Handbook
Objects purloined from my Father.
Pocket knife
Machette
Hatchet
Screwdriver and pliers

CHAPTER 16

GOODBYE TO SELF

It's been a pretty good run, almost a lifetime, but now it's time to part. Don't be hurt; I'm grateful. You got me through a fatherless childhood and helped me survive a mother who co-opted my dreams for hers. You taught me to ignore the people around me; they would have slowed me down and set me back.

Unfettered with guilt, I attended an expensive high school and college without concern for its impact on family finances and my sisters doing without.

Remember that pretty girl in El Paso? She loved me, but you made sending her a "dear John" letter easy. It wasn't time for me to acquire a wife; it would have added complications. I did such a good job that I saved a copy of the letter. It was one of your proudest moments. Later, when it was time, I installed a wife without considering that she might have her dreams. Too many compromises would have impeded my success. You taught me that.

I have many accomplishments: jobs, sports, and building an airplane — it's a long list — long because I didn't need to think about the needs of others. We put my career first and moved the family around the country. Why not? A man needs to earn a living, doesn't he? If there was any twinge of doubt, you were there to help me see things through my eyes, not there's.

You helped me get back to sleep when the babies were crying, reminding me that I needed rest — my job was more important. And when those babies went to college and then dropped out, we were silent, thinking about all that money saved, money for a bigger house or a new car.

A lifetime of saying, "I feel your pain, and I'd like to help, but I'm pretty busy right now," gets noticed, and lately, I've been trying to hide you by carefully planned acts of spontaneous giving.

But it's not working; you're showing again. Like the skydiver falling ever closer to the ground, I need to pull the ripcord and open my canopy before it's too late, before there's no one there when I land. You've stayed too long.

My cat and I made this decision, sitting in our small rented apartment, surrounded by strangers and cheap furniture. I hope you understand...

It's nothing personal.

CHAPTER 17

FINDING HAPPINESS LATE IN LIFE

Acceptance

Letting Go

Connection

The kids are raised, you are retired, you may be in your last house and car, and your life choices have narrowed to what day to go food shopping.

You may have significant health issues. Your doctor may have told you nothing can be done.

To varying degrees, everyone late in life is experiencing some form of loss, disappointment, helplessness, and lack of hope that anything will change. In this seemingly dark phase of your life, it may seem like there is no way to achieve happiness.

Your hand has been dealt, and you still have cards on the table, but how you play them will determine what happiness you may experience for the rest of your life. A friend may suggest talk therapy. You think, what else is there? No pill, no change of venue, and no starting over are possible.

It has always been true, but more so late in life, that it's not the objective facts in your life - health, income, loving relationships, etc. - but how you view them. As never before, you are challenged to process the good and the bad and find ways to accept where you are, let go of all the many components of your life you cannot change, and use your remaining time to discover (or rediscover) connections with people.

At first blush, this "life formula" could be printed and taped to your refrigerator door, and there isn't much more to say. Follow these rules, and you will be happy.

Well-meaning friends may offer pithy gems like, "just get over it, stop brooding, smell the roses, and so on." They either lack the intelligence to know it's not that simple, or they offer pithy advice so they can walk away.

In the absence of good professional help (I recommend), starting now, there are ways that you can move in a better direction. It will require soul searching and taking responsibility for your life (maybe for the first time).

ACCEPTANCE

If pragmatism could rule the day, acceptance would be easy. "What is done is done," my mother would say. There is no way to revisit your life choices and change the outcome. It's that simple. Most people know that, but going back to make imagined changes is not their motivation. What is taking you back, again and again, is that your "bad" choices suggest your future will be just as bad, maybe worse. So, endless time is spent analyzing the past, looking for the kernel of wisdom that will save you next time.

Decisions made in the past, viewed in the wisdom of your later years, can paint a dark picture of how you managed your life. Ruminating about them is the punishment you deserve, you think, for being so stupid. It's a subconscious self-flagellation that serves a purpose but not a good one. Worse, the mind has a way of stringing them together, every wrong decision, until you do not deserve to be happy.

Forgiveness is the key to acceptance. It may mean forgiveness for someone who harmed you, or it may, more likely, mean forgiving yourself. It opens the door to moving on because it removes the guilt and self-doubt that have become your prison. For example, the person you married 50 years ago has proven to be a wrong choice. You've made the best of it, but it was a bad decision. Try to revisit the moment you said yes to your marriage and understand that you were young, you had little life experience, and there may have been other forces acting on you. And, most importantly, you had no way to predict how this person would change or whom they would become. Forgive the person who did the best they could at that time. You.

Acceptance is not easy. It is a mountain you will climb every day. Doing that work is fuelled by knowing that your happiness is on the other side of acceptance. And every step you take in that direction will take you to a happier place.

LETTING GO

Letting go may seem like a component of acceptance, and it is, for the past. But it serves another purpose... for the present and the future. It may be easy to let go that you will not be a doctor or a famous person, etc. However, there may be some lingering thoughts ... if you had taken voice lessons and spent more time on academic subjects. For most people late in life, it is letting go-lives in the realm of small things. For example, you always wanted to garden and eat vegetables. To play an instrument. Any of these things may be possible, but the collection of many small items, unfulfilled, can become a burden and source of unhappiness. The ultimate is letting go of everything and then adding back the few things that are possible and fulfilling to you.

Like acceptance, letting go is not easy. It's an admission to yourself that life has not measured up to your expectations. And letting go becomes a list of your apparent failures. But was your list realistic? Or even possible?

In the end, the ultimate letting go is accepting that your life is not measured by what you have done or some imagined idea of what a person should be or could be. You fear that others will judge you, not for who you are, but for what you have not done. Be kind to yourself and avoid those people.

CONNECTION

People who win the lottery soon discover that it's never about the big thing, the win, but about the small things that gather around you, like flowers at your feet. Simple things will often bring the most pleasure. And the good news is that small pleasures are obtainable now. The big payoff may never come.

A good lesson to learn for people late in life, if you haven't already, is that the "things" that bring happiness are people, not objects. Your connection to people transcends anything material you can acquire.

The first step is taking an inventory of the people in your life and asking a tricky question. Are you spending time, paying attention, and cultivating relationships with these people? What are you doing to deepen these bonds to draw them closer to you? You are defined by what you pay attention to. Love and friendship show up in people's lives and let them know how important they are to you and how much you care.

We often take for granted people who love us and have been with us for a long time. They are on their journey too, and the signals you send may not align with your goal to have them close. Isolation through neglect of our people's connections is a common theme of aging. But it's easy to correct.

The first step is letting the people know you love them. Yes, they should know, but have you said the words? Have you said that you are glad they are in your life? Or should they know that? The connection "door" swings both ways. Paying attention to the people in your life draws them to you and fills your life with those critical connections.

It can be safely said that nothing else matters.

CHAPTER 18

LIFE DESCRIBED IN 75 WORDS

LIFE IS MOSTLY:
Sleeping
Working
Preparing, eating, and cleaning up from meals
Passively viewing entertainment or reading
Personal hygiene and grooming
Getting from point A to point B

LIFE IS SOMETIMES:
Loving
Hating
Hoping/dreaming
Being ill
Caring for others
Acquiring knowledge / being educated
Talking about and analyzing others
Praying to a higher power

LIFE IS RARELY:
Making love

Giving birth
Experiencing joy, happiness, ecstasy, sadness, grief, remorse, guilt, regret
Creating something original
Making restitution
Dying

CHAPTER 19

A LIFE HALF LIVED

When I look around at friends and family, why do I see sadness, simply making, and so little joy and laughter? Is it advancing age and the certainty of death that poisons our wells? Does life conspire to close the curtain after act two and leave us mouthing the words and moving on the stage behind a closed curtain? Can we blame our fate on poor genes, a bad marriage, or a bet on a horse that went lame on the backstretch? Are we the victims of a cosmic conspiracy of God and fate to make this life more accessible to leave when our time comes? Is our obituary written too early, waiting patiently in the hopper for our last breath, and then sent out to mourn a life that was only half lived? "He will be missed for a short while, but will soon be forgotten"—a truth can't be said.

When do we turn from hope and optimism to acceptance and its companion, despair? Is it after the last child is educated and the first grandchild is born that the road becomes meaningless? Have all the exciting stops been made, and the train is barreling to its final destination with us sitting like sphinxes, waiting?

The self-help book claiming "infinite possibilities" sits on the shelf, only half-read. We know better. It's another conspiracy to sell books and convince us to believe the answer lies somewhere in chapter 12, at the bottom of the page. But we can't get there; the mountains of author advice to take control, seize the day, and say no to failure loom ahead as insurmountable barriers. We can climb one hill, maybe two, but we're not Sisyphus. The rock is too big, too heavy, and we are too tired.

We are enjoined to "fight the good fight." But our armory is bare, and we have no moves left. Worse, we have no battle to fight because we have no goal in mind, no adversary to subdue. Death? I don't think so. Time with an imagined lover? That will not happen, and beating the cancer cells lurking in us? No, we are its host; it will take time to show us who's boss. The oncologist will have a sad expression when he delivers the sober news, his mind on his tennis game after work. You knew it would happen; it's not a surprise. You thank him and release him to his game.

Christmas will pass without a tree; Thanksgiving goes on without side dishes. Cookies aren't baked anymore. Friends recite their blood work results and how they cope with insomnia and a twitching leg. The internet becomes a feeding trough for pithy sayings, cartoons about aging, and stories that start, "You won't believe what happens after the ..." You trade them with your friends and pass them around like talismans for the aging. You tell your grandchildren you grew up without TV, and they don't know what you are talking about.

And when you stop caring about how you look and don't laugh at the cartoons, it no longer matters if you're on the stage. The new actors are waiting impatiently in the wings for you to leave. Your run is over, and the audience doesn't care either; they're anxious to see what's next.

CHAPTER 20

THE MAN BEFORE YOU

Pity the man before you, naked, vulnerable, and wanting only your mercy. Pulled from his mother's breast, tossed into the world, and told to be strong and show no emotion. His father taught him to fight, to bow to no man, and make his way in a competitive and dark world.... alone.

Trusting no one, he hides his insecurity and presents a brave face to everyone. No man will know his inner heart, but you do now.

And when you lie down with him and feel his beating heart, all his fears vanish, the doors fly open, and you have taken him back to a warm place he barely remembers.

Pity the naked man standing before you, all he wants is your love and this moment of transcendence.

CHAPTER 21

TIME TO MOVE ON

Many folks (like me) from humble or disadvantaged backgrounds (like me) who achieve a modicum of success (like me) often feel the need to wear their accomplishments like medals on a military uniform.

This medal is for building my airplane. This one is for installing detailed crown molding in a small condo. And so on. What is not said or admitted is that each "medal" has a reverse side, one that discloses that building an airplane made a five-year hole in my life and risked financial ruin, that the crown molding and other condo fix-ups consumed years of my life, years not spent enjoying nature or reading a good book.

The need to prove myself is a burden that has never been lifted. Good haircuts and fixed teeth don't entirely remove the delusional stigma of feeling unworthy or not being fully accomplished. Every encounter is an opportunity to steer the conversation to my credentials, and the "medals" proves I am a worthwhile individual. "I went to school with Barry Goldwater Jr. and John Dean" demonstrates that you walked with best. You might say, "John wasn't that smart," and get a laugh and a nod of envy for your good fortune.

I carry my vida everywhere and present it with the slightest provocation. I graduated from Carnegie Mellon and worked at Apple and HP. You *must* see me as a person who has overcome a rough start, a humble beginning.

Like an anorexic, standing in a mirror and seeing a fat person, I can never pile the evidence high enough to feel that I have made it, that you will accept me as an equal.

A man lost in the desert will instinctively discard objects he is carrying, making thoughtful decisions about what is needed and what is not. It's a telescoping process until the oasis is reached or the journey is unexpectedly over - death. At age 81, I am still trying to hold on to everything ... and it's not working. I mistakenly think anything I let go of is a sure sign that my incomplete life is over.

I've decided it's time to move on. I want to discard "objects" to lighten my burden and make the journey easier. Such decisions do not come quickly for a man who spent his whole life displaying "medals" of his worth. It will require me to discard that final aspect of my life that I hold so tightly - the belief that I must prove to you that I am worthwhile. It was never the case; I didn't have the wisdom to know that ... until now.

To start, I want to live where I am and in the present moment. I'm canceling all the email connections to my past life in San Jose. To my former retirement community. To the bike club in California. To the amber alerts and power outage notifications. And to LinkedIn, a connection to my working life from more than a dozen years ago.

I'm removing the Palo Alto license plate holders from my cars. I live in Weaverville now. Moving here was in the past. I won't open every conversation with, "I'm new; we moved here from California." I won't compare the cost of a meal or the availability of organic food (or anything) with California. California is over.

And here is a list of my new "rules of the road:"

I won't talk about building an airplane unless it's with a fellow pilot.
I won't say I worked at Apple, HP, etc. unless asked.
I won't volunteer my age out of the blue.
I won't say I'm a vegetarian at the meat counter or to the checkout clerk.

I won't say I just moved here.

I won't say I went to Staunton Military Academy unless it's in a conversation about schools.

I won't say I traveled to Japan, England, France, or Holland as a young engineer unless it's in a travel conversation.

I won't say I'm in perfect health, ever.

I wouldn't say I was in the Army unless I talked to a fellow soldier.

I wouldn't say I once rode a bicycle 100 miles a week unless it was with a fellow bike rider.

I won't walk away from anyone unless it's clear we are done talking.

CHAPTER 22

PERMISSION TO SPEAK FREELY, SIR?

That line is heard in Hollywood war movies, not the military. A solder can *never* speak freely, and indeed, not with impunity. I'm not a soldier anymore, and I can say what I want. Unless you live in North Korea, Russia, or third-world countries, you can always speak your mind. No permission is needed. But that's not precisely the point. You can talk freely, but it's unlikely that anyone will want to listen, or has the time to listen, or will ever see your words on the screen of their computing device. In the global internet age, we ironically find ourselves more isolated and unheard than ever.

There was a time when our voice was lucky to travel a hundred yards down a country road. Now it can circle the globe in seconds ... along with a "cloud" of other voices/words that will most likely settle, along with yours, as dust on the side of the digital highway. Nothing has changed since solitary man lived in caves (old cave drawings have a better chance of being seen than the words you write today).

What is the point? I am one of seven billion, four hundred million persons (Alexa gave me that fact) on the planet. How can I expect that my voice, my words, should be heard by anyone or rise to the level of needing to be heard? We are lost in a sea of humanity. Consider it's a sunny day on the beach, and a baby poops in the ocean. Babies, do that. It's unlikely the beach will be cleared, or the sea drained. Why? Our microscopic impact on the planet is too localized and insignificant to move beyond the tiny bubble of our existence.

Exceptions like the works of Shakespeare or the words in the Declaration of Independence won't sway my opinion. They offer me little hope that anyone will see the next word I type on my keyboard: "I n v I s I b l e."

Examples abound. Take the 1957 Pulitzer prize-winning book, "Profiles in Courage," allegedly written by President Kennedy but by his speech writer, Ted Sorensen. Whatever it had to say, no matter how insightful or significant, had a short arc of attention and quickly faded into obscurity. No one mentions the book, checks it out of the library, or cites a passage to make a point.

Barrack Obama's July 24, 2008 speech in Berlin regarding the Berlin Wall was a once-in-a-century message for all men and women to hear. Yet, who has read or heard it? Its significance faded quickly, maybe in days, and has only now returned (not the words) as a foil to counteract Trump's call for a US border wall.

An experiment you can do at home: write a novel and publish it. Pour your heart and soul into the story, give it life, and research the nuances and subtleties of characters that become alive in your imagination. Learn the twists and turns of self-publishing. Please give it a snappy cover and flyleaf. When the proof arrives, turn it page by page and see how it differs from a Simon and Schuster book. It isn't. Then find a way to accept that, at best, one or two dozen people on our planet of 7 billion, 400 million will ever read the book. Less than that number will even mention that they have read it or provide any feedback on how it had significance for them.

And so, having labeled me an invisible man, and In the face of my cosmic anonymity, I now permit myself to speak freely at age 78. I could wait until 80 and use the significance of being 80 as permission to do just about anything. "Officer, I'm 80, and there were no bathrooms around." But why wait? I may not be here to celebrate my 80th birthday. There is something about facing one's death that lends a sense of urgency, and time is running out, but to do what? Such a question inevitably leads to questions about what life is for and why I am here. Here's my sobering reality. I've not conquered cancer, solved world hunger, or laid down any marker that alters the course of human destiny in any way. I'm left with the usual obituary-style summation of ordinary life: Born in Clairton, PA on December 3, 1939; married Jeanne Cook on October 9, 1965, and fathered two sons, Mark and Matthew." Anything more detailed would not pass the two-second attention span of those reading. "Click," and it's gone. It's hard to accept that it may come down to a binary description of my life, for example, "he was a good man."

In my teenage years, our family-owned a boxer dog. He was appropriately named "King." Not an intelligent dog, he nevertheless protected our Watson estate until he could no longer stand. He did his best to keep newspapers from being delivered, and when off duty, he mostly ate and slept. King wore a collar from early doghood. He accepted the real and psychological burden of being constrained by that collar. He didn't think about it (if dogs can think) in later life. I found that out when I removed his collar for some reason, I can't remember. He was in distress and maneuvered his head back into the collar as best he could. It seemed odd at the time. Freedom was offered, but he chose the familiar and the safe.

Today, I find myself much like King, and the scary part, in ways I don't fully understand. Every human walking the planet wears a collar, and for a good reason, you might say. Our parents do their best to create safe ways for us to think and act, and in their mind, a way to make sure we travel through life getting along and, importantly, to be successful. Without thinking about it or even being aware, we wear an extensive collection of cultural and societal rules and constraints. The list is comprehensive. And religion piles on, too. Don't eat meat on Friday. Attend mass on Sunday or risk not being with God in heaven. Women must wear scarves when in public. If you live in a conservative neighborhood and want to be accepted, there's a long list of rules and behaviors to be carefully followed. The consequences are more than shunning; it could be dead in some parts of the world.

Permitting myself to speak, and by extension, permission to remove the dog collar at a time when most folks are signing medical directives is fraught with a long list of potential unintended consequences. Or... maybe not. Who will hear?

I am speaking out with my collar-less truths:

1. We are killing the planet, and there is no turning back or any prospect that we (the global "we") will hold the destruction in check. We are well past the tipping point. Your sons and daughters will not have a better life than you; we are past that.
2. The United States could be better in the world. Allen Sorkin captured it best when actor Jeff Bridges was asked that question in a Newsroom vignette. It's impossible to draw a definitive conclusion, but for a moment, open your mind to how awful we have been since our country's founding and continuing to this day.
3. There are no golden years in old age—a year at best. Medical advances will keep you alive, maybe too long, as you watch your body degrade and fail, part by part.
4. Most people lie. It's in our DNA. It may be small, or it may be big, but we can't help ourselves. If someone tells your "something," consider that it may be a lie. See how long *you* can go between lies.
5. We do not live in a democracy and haven't for a long time. Just because you vote, don't conclude it proves we have a democracy. It doesn't. Our government has long been co-opted by special interests, big business, and political charlatans that keep you ignorant and ill-informed. Your vote to end abortion and create a small government has taken you out of the middle class and put you on the welfare rolls, ironically, by the politicians who also want to take that from you.

6. Barack Obama was born a US citizen. If you voted for someone who denies this, what does that say about your ability to rationalize just about anything?
7. Six (some say seven) percent of Catholic priests are pedophiles. If you have kids, think about those odds and how they may impact you. Watch the movie "Spotlight." It's not fiction. Google the details of the funeral given to Cardinal Law by the Vatican.
8. Most organized religion is fiction and the invention of man (specifically, by males). If you believe in God and believe you were given even the slightest measure of intelligence, try to analyze organized religion in any logical way. You will run into thousands of brick walls adorned with the sign: "have faith." If you accept that God created the flawed humans we are, why would He do that? Is it some heavenly experiment to populate a planet and see how we get along? News flash: we don't get along and kill each other in large numbers. Does that make sense, or are you asking me to have faith because we don't understand His ways?
9. Our diet is killing us. I penned the title for an essay I wrote, "Death by legal ingestion." The tragedy of early death and the societal burden of enormous healthcare costs overshadows the cuteness of this title. Yes, we can afford to eat food that is bad for us, and we do it in increasingly more significant quantities. The production of this lousy food places an unsustainable burden on our environmental system. Take a road trip and visit a hog farm, a chicken farm, a dairy farm, and a cattle farm and observe what they have in common. In reality, however, you will never be permitted to enter. It's that bad. We don't need a scientific/medical breakthrough to solve this problem. The answer is known but largely ignored.
10. Many white Americans will never accept that skin color does not matter, and as a nation, we will continue to exhibit subtle and sometimes overt acts of prejudice. The following words, taken from the constitution, are not valid and never have been, "We

hold these truths to be self-evident, that **all men are created equal**, that their Creator endows them with certain unalienable Rights, that among these are Life, Liberty and the Pursuit of Happiness." Look in the mirror; if you are white, breathe a sigh of relief. The constitution was written for you.

11. The "end game" will not be pretty. Whatever semblance of a civil and safe society we have, of a life where we have a measure of control, is vanishing right before our eyes, bit by bit. A Tom Waite song captured an essential truth, *"It's the same with men as with horses and dogs. Nothing wants to die."* That elemental reality will overrule our basic humanity when conditions push the globe closer and closer to the edge of survival. Offshore bank accounts, security guards, bulletproof cars, and gated communities will not save you; delay the inevitable. Like overeating, eating lousy food, overeating alcohol, ignoring the body's need for exercise, etc., the end game will not kill you today or tomorrow; it will take a while. It's a slow death. With luck, you will not be here.

CHAPTER 23

I RESIGN; IT'S YOUR TURN

I resign. Yes, at age 73, I decided to pack it in. No, not on life, but any responsibility I bear for the state of the world. I haven't done an excellent job in my lifetime, and now it's clear that Sisyphus needs to give up. That rock will not budge on what's left of my watch. It's your turn. Shoulder up!

In the lead-up to the Vietnam War, I was assigned to Germany and drank beer, and drove my sports car around Europe. I did my two years, got out, never looked back, never looked at the newsreels of death and carnage, and never joined a peace march. When civil rights demonstrations and protests were held and people were killed in Mississippi, I hid in my work as an engineer. And now, late in life, with work and children raised, and finally having eyes wide open to the sad blight of the world, I find my ability to dent the fabric of the universe out of my grasp. Oh, I'll still do small acts of kindness and look for volunteer jobs to give something back, but the heavy lifting that's up to you.

Here are the significant issues (a baker's dozen) that I'm turning over to you:

Gay marriage. Two people who love each other should be able to marry. I'm tired of hearing "bible" arguments about the alleged harm it would do to me. Slavery was a tradition in the south. Enough! Maybe someone will put down their bible and listen to *you*.

Rising ocean levels and global warming. People who think science is not in or that the earth is 6,000 years old annoy me and should be barred from attending bible school. They seem good Christians; they may want to get to heaven sooner. I live 105 feet above sea level, so I'm okay for my lifetime.

Deforestation of the Amazon. So, third-world people want to clear the land and raise crops to feed their families. We pillaged the ground and killed most Indians here; it's hard for us to be sanctimonious about it. Maybe we should help you (find another way).

Animal extinction. Tinkering with the delicate balance of nature doesn't seem like a good idea. Commercial raising of hogs with hundreds of animals per acre doesn't either. Need Rhino horns to help your sex life? Better solve this one right away.

Gridlocked and dysfunctional government. Can you imagine flying a spaceship and there is only one control? Okay, that is what we have, the vote. I've tried, but I think we're f---ed.

I am shrinking middle class. I've tried my best not to shrink. Unfortunately, the wealthy 1% have more votes and influence than you or I. This has been going on (the decline) for 30 years. Maybe we need more data? More food stamps? More soup kitchens?

Global terrorism. I'm done with the Bush "war on terrorism." I don't know any terrorists, and I don't want to spend any of my precious time left looking for one.

Poverty. Since we have yet to tackle to root cause of poverty, why start now? Even if I gave away all my money, the statistic wouldn't budge. You can choose to ignore it at your own risk. Buy a house in a gated community.

Crime. I didn't, but you can join a neighborhood watch group and carry "heat." It might be better (just my advice) to support lowering the cost of education and job training—just a thought.

Fox news. I'm okay with keeping it around. It will remind everyone (not watching Fox news) how ignorant and uninformed a large number of people are (see 13), below). Also, if your kids have trouble with school grades, those folks will keep the test scores low.

Stupid wars that don't make us safer. I did my two years in the military, and nothing good came of it, so I suggest you support a measure that would move the congressional buildings to Kandahar, Afghanistan. I think that would be an essential education for the older men who send our young men and women to die in strange places.

Oppression of women. This category includes female sexual mutilation, rape, forced illiteracy, slavery, and unequal status (driving a car, etc.). All I can say is set a good example and be careful where you vacation with your daughters. See ignorant people, 13) below.

Ignorant people. Since the discovery of fire and low-cost prescription glasses, Darwin's natural selection has been thwarted. There's everywhere, quoting the bible when it suits their agenda, voting on a single issue like abortion, trying to eliminate the teaching of science in schools, thinking that the wealthy will create jobs if they just had lower taxes, and the list goes on. Learn to live with it, as I did. With education funding drying up, it's only going to get worse.

Missing from the list: keeping Lake Tahoe blue, protecting birds from blade strikes in a wind farm, clean water, etc. You can't do everything; leave a list for your kids.

CHAPTER 24

LEARNING ABOUT SEX IN A SUPERMARKET CHECKOUT LINE

My supermarket is stadium-size, but only three checkout lines are open. It's a sign of the economic times: staff cutbacks and price increases. I couldn't be happier, at least about the cutbacks. The long lines block the cross isles and snake into the shopping area. It takes some maneuvering to join the longest streak. I hope the checkout person is wearing a "Trainee" badge; it will give me a little more time.

Thankful that I don't have a purse or kids, I abandon the cart and head to the checkout station, stopping at the rack of newspapers and magazines. I skip the magazine with a grainy picture of Britney Spears, wearing no makeup and five extra pounds, and look for the latest copy of Cosmopolitan or Redbook. There it is; the bold type rivets my attention: "35 Ways to Please your Man." America may have lost interest in stories about space aliens impregnating helpless earthlings or stories of giant watermelons the size of a Volkswagen Beetle — maybe we're too sophisticated now. Still, there's no flagging of interest in sex. Last month I read: "It's Winter, Turn up the Heat in the Bedroom." My supermarket is a stand-up version of the Christian Science Monitor Reading Room, with sex as the universal religion. I glance at the checkout clerk, a teenager wearing jeans and a supermarket logo tee shirt; her hands blur as she shuffles the items past a laser bar code reader, then heads back to my cart with my reading material. The line is moving too fast; a gap is forming ahead of my cart. Regrettably, technology has vanquished the thirtyish, single mom making ends meet, perky uniform with nice hair and nails checkout clerk; they were slower and friendlier.

I'm on to the magazine publishers. The "35 Ways . . ." title is nowhere to be found in the table of contents. I know it has been renamed and is buried under one of the Department headings. Like the supermarket, they want me to browse the "isles" of the magazine to find the article, stopping at each advertiser along the way. I know it's not page 30; it's more likely to be on page 168. I make the match and head there, the blown-in inserts falling to the floor like white leaves.

I'm not surprised; the article is disappointing. I know 10-12 ways would be more than enough for a man, but 35 will sell more magazines. I conclude that the author hasn't been down the road too far. Maybe she's a newly minted English major from Bryn Mawr or Radcliffe, clever to a fault at turning a phrase, single, living in New York, and dating a Hollywood-handsome young man that's not ready to settle down just yet. Sitting at her computer and recalling sex scenes from books in her required undergraduate reading, she quickly gets to twenty ways. And with complete knowledge of sex since the beginning of humanity, only one Google click away, she reaches the 35 goals.

In recent years the articles have gotten shorter and shorter. I won't be surprised when I see "LOL" and "BWL" in the text. Sex is losing (or has lost) its nuance and subtlety. The articles are like the no-frills, get to the point IKEA instructions to assemble a dresser, with a few twists: "for variety, try inserting part "B" into part "D" instead of part "C." I may be old fashioned. Still, I think the magazine advice should pass the "beaver test," as in "Leave it to Beaver." It may be bad advice if I can't imagine June Cleaver in a skimpy maid's outfit greeting Ward at the door. It is rejected if I can't imagine Ward's crumpled business suit and briefcase beside the bed.

Now at the checkout station, I close the magazine and place it over the not yet ready for a comeback image of Britney, and smile at the checkout clerk.

CHAPTER 25

STUCK IN SECOND GEAR

A life not fully lived.

Growing up in the fifties, cars that my family could afford had manual transmissions: three gears to go forward and one for reverse. Nothing was automatic, but then, nothing appeared complicated ... until the idea of a clutch was introduced. It had to be in at times and out and slipped when starting.

And so, at some point in my teenage life, I had to learn those gears, how to use the clutch, and take those first steps toward adulthood. Driving was my passage to independence. And for my parents, their passage from being a chauffeur to living with the possibility of a disaster ahead. It could be a car crash or a lapse of judgment at a drive-in movie. Either could change our lives forever.

Cousins or uncles made the best driving instructor; they had more patience and had less at stake. With the engine running, the transmission is in first, and the clutch is slowly let out. But not knowing when it begins to engage was an engine-stalling mystery that had to be learned. Bucking starts led to a jerky, surging ride, with the added responsibility of steering the car.

First gear was necessary to get going, like a push to my flexible flyer sled. It wasn't helpful for anything but to allow shifting to second. In and out with the clutch. Shift. No finesse was required. And soon, I was circling the church parking lot with abandon. The car and my cousin began to relax and believe my driving was possible.

I'm a driver now, but still in second gear and still in the parking lot. It was comfortable, and I felt I could control the car and my progress. A nudge on the gas pedal to go faster; release and the vehicle would slow down. One of the essential driving ingredients, using the brakes, was not needed or used.

To earn my freedom and to leave the parking lot to start my life meant shifting to third gear, but I was afraid I would lose control and crash. Staying in second gear wasn't an option; I knew that, but I tried to delay the final turn to the exit and the highway for as long as possible I was stuck in second gear.

The distant memory of that last shift to third gear has long faded. Soon my teenage impatience wanted third and the freedom to speed down the road, going as fast as possible. I loved every new girlfriend thoroughly and was ready to spend the rest of my life with her. I left the rocky bank of the Monongahela river and swam to the other side with no one to save me. I read the "electricity" section of a 1939 encyclopedia and began fixing vacuum tube radios. I was moving at full speed.

Looking back, I'd like to say that I left that church parking lot and stayed in third gear for the rest of my life. Yet, so many times, and sometimes without knowing it, I fell back to the security of second and returned to the control I felt I needed to steer safely. A life in third at full speed can be seen as reckless. So much can be lost by flying off the road at the next curve. Is a life fully lived judged by how far you get down the street or how well you enjoyed the journey? There is no simple answer to that question. But it helps to be aware of those choices and make decisions that keep us moving forward sustainably. There may be times when you need to go flat-out and times when you need to proceed cautiously. Making those decisions consciously is the key ingredient to a life fully lived.

Now, late in my life, It's understandable that folks like me want to put on the brakes. The danger is everywhere... a fall, a turn in the wrong direction. I, too, feel that urge to live my last days in comfortable gear. However, I wake up every day fighting that feeling. I've come this far. With still some miles to go, I choose to keep my foot on the gas, to continue roller skating and riding my bicycle, and to continue being open to new challenges ... to the end of the road.

CHAPTER 26

SUPERMAN AND WONDER WOMAN CAN'T HELP YOU

As children, we are drawn to the strength and power of superheroes like Wonder Woman and Superman. At a time when we are increasingly aware of our vulnerability and the dangers of the larger world, we are constantly confronted with the limitations of being a child and having almost no power. And so the unlimited strength of these characters is both transcendent and satisfying. We have learned that evil exists in the world, but it can be overcome by the superhuman force of characters dedicated to making everything safe. Mom and dad can't stop a sinister person from setting out to destroy the world, but Superman can. We believe the world is safer with Superman and Wonder Woman in our lives.

That frame of reference can remain with us well into adulthood until we learn that our heroes can only exist in a world of pure good and pure evil, and unfortunately, our lives are not like that. Archetype villains rarely exist, and more importantly, the help from single-dimensional, all-powerful characters does not map into the real-world nuance and ambiguity we encounter. Wonder Woman never has to puzzle whether a villain is worthy of her intervention; Superman never pauses before stopping a speeding train or catching a man falling from the roof. The "villains" in our real lives are more likely to be our spouse, boss, relatives, and rarely the man in the street with a gun. What to do, then?

Many times there is no simple answer. Our hero's physical strength does not help solve our problem; it's another strength that is needed, but it is rarely portrayed in the simplistic world of comics and cartoons. Even the bully on the playground in our childhood eventually had to find another way to shape their will. Our demons and enemies live at our house, work, or in the public domain of politicians, CEOs, judges, or juries. And whether personal or political, their view of right and wrong can collide with ours, and there is no way to call Superman and have him find a phone booth to change (today, it would be a cubicle or kiosk) and come to our rescue.

Lacking someone to save us, we muster our strength, take personal responsibility, buoy our resolve with self-help books, get advice from friends, and eventually muddle through our problems. Effecting change may be possible, and we are often left with the nobility of the long road of acceptance and suffering. And yet we never stop wanting to be saved by someone or something. It would be silly to look for a real-life Superman, but plausible to look for an "adult" version of the man-of-steel. That vision lurks in our concept of God, the ultimate superpower, who can save a dying child, turn back the angry sea, and deliver the glory of heaven. He can do anything if He chooses to. Given a necessary ingredient of faith, the story of His existence is no more or less plausible than Superman's journey to the earth from a dying planet. However, unlike many of our petitions to God, if Superman knew you were in trouble, help would be given. It would be that simple. In our adult world, God is elusive and sometimes capricious, and His help defies any pulpit explanation of exactly how or when it will come about.

Despite the myths, we unconsciously respond to those who claim superpower status and promise to save us. It could be the company that rescues you from house foreclosure, the person who can "make you over to look beautiful," the doctor who can cure your cancer, the pill that will prevent a heart attack, or ultimately, the politician that will save Medicare and eliminate the national debt in four years. These modern-day superpowers tap into that child-like part of us that wants to believe we can be saved. They offer hope, even if it is illusory.

Superman and Wonder Woman can't help you; take comfort that if they existed, they would often be mired in the same kinds of problems you are having. It's okay to keep looking, but face your issues with your own "Superman" strength. That's what they would do.

CHAPTER 27

PERSPECTIVE IS WORTH 10 IQ POINTS

I first heard this at Apple Computer in the eighties, spoken by Alan Kay, a research scientist. It was a heady time for innovation and a vibrant time for advancing the frontier of consumer-level computing. He reminded us that it's not just pure brainpower but the context or "perspective" of problem-solving and innovation that counts too. He may have also said: "the urinal at New York airport is smarter than your computer; it knows when you are standing in front of it and when you leave." It's still true today. I was glad to hear his remarks as I constantly felt at least 10 IQ points behind that crowd.

Do I have the answer? Perspective? No, it's always running a little ahead of me, like the rabbit at a dog track. I keep running, but the race will be over before I catch it, if ever. Meanwhile, the days rush past, one blending into another. There are very few markers in a retired person's life. Births, weddings, and birthdays are all transitory events with a short half-life, wedged between tomorrow and yesterday, hardly making an impression. What gets our attention? It's deaths and the continuing decline of our physical bodies. We carry a running list of our friends and relatives, people who have "passed." Passed to what?

The media loves to note the birthday of dead people and to dip into their secret archives of obituaries for living people who are now dead.

Lacking a "good" war or news about the reversal of global warming, we spend days and weeks hearing about Michael Jackson. I prefer an excellent crap overhearing a word about his life. One day of coverage would empty my cup.

Back to perspective. Did you ever take a plane ride, look out the window, a temporary prisoner in your seat, and believe that you suddenly knew what everything meant? You knew what was essential and, even better, what was unnecessary. I have, so many times. But when the plane door opened and the "let me be the first to welcome you to Pittsburgh' was announced, the perspective floated out that door. Poof! By the time I got to the baggage, the memory of it was gone, and I was thinking about the rental car and how to get to the hotel.

CHAPTER 28

THANKS FOR THE HEART ATTACK

Like the well-worn expression, "thanks, I needed that," I look upon my recent heart attack as a gift. It may sound facetious of me, being one of the lucky seven out of ten that survives a heart attack, but I have experienced a positive outcome that I would have never expected, and I am grateful.

To understand how I arrived at this perspective, it's necessary to digress a bit. I was one of those who sailed through life with nothing more severe than a case of the sniffles. I was one of the blessed ones whose genetics and lifestyle set me apart from the "rest" of the population. I listened patiently while friends discussed (it seems for hours) their various ailments and had little to add to the conversation. I tried to be humble but secretly believed that staying thin, eating a moderate diet, and exercising vigorously gave me a free pass from their physical afflictions.

For 72 years, I ran, played racquetball, rode a bicycle, and roller skated without thinking my life would ever be curtailed. Friends and family called me "superman," saying I would outlive my friends and family. I believed them and found ways to keep proving it to myself by taking on more excellent and significant physical challenges. Two weeks before my heart attack, I rode my bicycle in a metric century:

100 KM (67 miles) in a single day of riding that included 6,120 feet of hill climbing. It was difficult, but I was addicted to the pain of pushing myself to the limit of my body's performance, and I wore my pain like laurel leaves.

Several weeks later, imagine my surprise when 20 miles into a "short" 32-mile club ride, I experienced deep pain in the center of my chest, like a severe case of indigestion. I had no reason to suspect that plaque had broken loose and caused a clot that produced a 90% blockage of an artery feeding blood to my heart. It was nothing like I had ever experienced before, so I continued riding as I waited for the pain to subside. It didn't. Soon I was within 100 yards of the Stanford Hospital emergency room. Yet I continued riding, getting weaker by the mile. I knew something was wrong but had no reason to think HEART ATTACK. Something in the back of my mind knew what it was, a faint warning voice, but I continued in a state of denial. The desire to get home was overwhelming; stopping and calling 911 would have been an acknowledgment that I was no longer superman, no longer a person "above" the rest of the population.

I rode the ten miles back to my car and then the 10-minute drive to my home.

The pain persisted as I lay on the bed, and it began to sink in that I had a heart attack. A Google search for symptoms confirmed it. I changed clothes, took two aspirins, drove myself to the emergency room of El Camino Hospital, carefully parked my car, and then, holding my Kaiser medical card in my hand, told the nurse, "I think I have a heart attack."

The rest was in a blur; the EKG, the confirmation that yes, it was a heart attack, the trip to the cath lab, the insertion of a stent at the blockage site, and the doctor later telling me that I may need a bypass operation. I was in shock. Had he confused me with another patient, maybe someone who smoked and was overweight?

The pain stopped minutes after arriving at the ER when a Nitrostat pill was inserted under my tongue. From then on, and even today, I have experienced no pain or discomfort from a heart attack. It's strange to have such a significant medical condition and feel no physical discomfort. Did I have a heart attack? I'll have to trust the volley of tests that were conducted (and continue to be conducted) that indicate various percentage blockages to arteries feeding my heart. But I can see why so many people have heart attacks, have a stent inserted, and then go on to live their lives the same way. Not me; I had decided (and been given an ultimatum from my wife) that I would change my diet ... and what else? More exercise? The idea was ludicrous; I would probably have to do less exercise (or more age-appropriate exercise).

After being released from the hospital, my new life began with a salad. While I was stirring the salad with my fork, looking for non-existent pieces of chicken or salmon, it was decided that my plaque-clogged arteries needed help, and the answer was a diet change. There would be no meat, no salt, no sugar, no dairy, no processed foods, and no saturated fat in my diet. That was just the beginning. Books were purchased and quickly surveyed for dietary information. Books with author names like John McDougall, Joel Furhman, Colin Campbell, and Caldwell Esselstyn rose in a pile on the coffee table. I would eat nothing white, and I wouldn't eat anything that had a face or a mom and dad. I would eat a plant-based diet.

Watching the documentary "Forks above Knives," I slowly absorbed the fact that the Western diet is killing us, and it's a conspiracy spawned by the medical profession (in a gentle but negligent way), the FDA, the pharmaceutical industry, and the vast dairy, cattle, and agro-industries. And all of this bad food is being served to us on the shelves of supermarkets, the glossy products overloaded with nutrient-stripping processing, excess sugar, salt, and unnecessary calories and fat. And it isn't our fault; we have been conditioned from birth to crave this food, and it's a big business—more significant than anyone can imagine. With the government's blessing, the food industry delivers the food for this lousy diet, and the medical and drug industry has the pill that will fix the consequences, and no one dares challenge the status quo. And for the most part, as a nation, we are a party to this conspiracy because this food is what we want... or have been taught to enjoy.

It would sink in later that in becoming a vegan, I had passed through a nutritional portal where there was no turning back. As my digestion struggled to adjust to a plant-based diet, gurgling, cramping, and always being near a bathroom, my intellect struggled to absorb this new knowledge. I was a recovering meat addict and in a state of withdrawal.

Unsurprisingly, I constantly channeled my mother's fried chicken or a white pasta dish laden with a soppy concoction of salty tomato sauce and meatballs in the first few weeks. And then, slowly, at first, things started to change...

First, I had to realize that if I continued to watch documentaries made with hidden cameras capturing animal cruelty, and if I continued my endless browsing of the web for evidence of the restorative benefit of a vegan diet, I would trade my previous addiction to excessive levels of exercise for a new habit: the crusade to change the American diet. I had to let that go.

In the ensuing weeks, a feeling of well-being swept over me—the daily naps disappeared—and my weight was plummeting, sometimes over a pound a day. My taste was heightened; in the absence of salt and butter, I started to taste the vegetables and nuts I was eating in large quantities. I ate until I burst and then literally gorged on a "dessert" of Mellon, strawberries, fresh pineapple, or white nectarines. And my weight continued to drop, eventually leveling off (as was predicted by the vegan "bibles") at close-to-normal BMI—nearly twenty-five pounds from my pre-MI weight. The belly I previously held in for photographs was gone! I imagined the fat around my heart was also gone, and that put a smile on my face. Another smile came when I bought new jeans with a waist size two inches smaller than my pre-vegan self.

There were other benefits. My life had slowed down. Daily walks opened up a new visual and fragrant world I was missing on my bicycle. Instead of thinking about the next hill to climb, the considerable effort to maintain my bicycling speed and keep up with my friends, I was thinking about how joyful and relaxing it was to slow down and "smell the roses," as my mother always cautioned me to do. I will go back to bicycling; I know that, but it will never be the same.

Looking back at this life-changing experience, I realize that my heart attack gave me a chance to re-examine who I was and what I valued; it was a time-out and a wakeup call to understand that a human "superman" can experience a sharp pain in the chest that signals (if you're lucky enough to survive) that it's time to make some significant life changes before it's too late.

Thanks, I needed that.

CHAPTER 29

THE SILENT GENERATION

World War II babies, now in their seventies, have been designated the "silent generation" (along with depression-era children). Too young to remember the details of the war years, old enough to avoid serving in Vietnam, they married, raised families, and have lived their lives under society's radar. As teens, they drank nickel cokes and listened to Doo-Wop music; soon, it was beer drinking and rock and roll, and later, when the Beetles hit the music scene, they were too old to embrace it as their own. Bob Dylan and folksingers with lyrics you could understand came along when they were raising their young children. They danced, drank cheap wine, and paid their mortgage faithfully every month. Mostly, they were out of sync with the major forces that shape today's world.

Living with instant messaging, 24-hour news, and a fountain of knowledge at our fingertips, the internet, it's hard to dial all this back and visualize the time for a child growing up in the forties and fifties. In small towns like mine, the porthole to the outside world was indeed small ... almost non-existent. For a moment, imagine the following: no public library (the bookmobile came later), no boy scout troop, no little league, no public swimming pool, no television (that came when I was ten years old), and no communication with the outside world other than the National Geographic Magazine and the radio in the living room. What about the school, you may ask? The textbooks of that time presented a world that might as well have been science fiction. Whatever connection it had with our lives was missing and not discussed.

It's also hard to imagine a parent of that time not being involved with their children and guiding them to a whole life. But for the most part, they had little involvement, and we moved through our childhood independently. I remember only two rules: be home on time for supper and not get into trouble.

My parents were people who remembered the depression and valued the privilege of working and having enough to eat. Many had just returned from the war and were anxious to restart their lives. They were enjoying the post-war housing boom, factory jobs, and the tranquility of a peaceful life. The battle, including the brief but costly Korean war, taught them that the outside world was dangerous and that it was their time to enjoy life. The kids would finish high school, get a good union job, raise a family, have a company pension, and nothing more was necessary... as long as they stayed out of "trouble." That's how I was raised, with one exception, and it turned out to be an important one; I was to go to college and get a job as a professional, a term my mom often used to describe a man who wore a necktie.

Looking back on this experience, I realize I was the last generation to grow up with complete freedom. By today's standards and with an understanding of the world we now live in, it's almost incomprehensible to believe that a child, not even a teenager, could leave the house in the morning and return at night for supper with the statement (often not needed), "I'm going out to play." It's also hard to imagine giving your son or daughter a B-B gun and, not much later, a 22 rifle as a toy to play with. As a ten-year-old, I knew the difference between 22 longs and shorts and ammunition that was bird shot, blunt, or hollow-tipped. By that time, I had killed hundreds of birds and blown up everything in my neighborhood (like mailboxes) with firecrackers supplied by my parents for the Fourth of July.

Aside from "arming me," almost nothing was given (Christmas train sets being an exception) in the way of toys or sports equipment. My bicycle was an old girl's bike. My ice skates were white girls' skates. Everything else I needed or wanted had to be created, and it was in that creation that we acquired life skills and learned what was safe and dangerous. As post-war children, and in the culture of blue-collar life, we knew it was permitted to kill animals—not a pet—if you wanted to and that somewhere in the world, people could also be killed if they were the "enemy." With this knowledge and our penknives, we created weapons and instruments to destroy things.

Take a young boy to a park, even one of today's sanitized, child-proof parks, and he will instinctively pick up a stone and throw it. Mom will quickly nip that behavior in the bud; eyes could be hit and people blinded. However, left alone, I quickly learned how to select a good "throwing rock." Size, shape, and weight mattered, and "Kentucky windage" needed to be applied to hit a stray dog on the move. Unsatisfied with the range and effort of rock throwing, a slingshot was required. They were proffered by ads in the back of our comic books from a company called "Wham-O." The picture was all we needed; a "Y" shaped tree branch and rubber bands cut from car tire inter-tubes were easy to make. Luckily, inter-tubes in the years after the war were made of natural rubber, unlike the synthetic rubber that came along later, something that was utterly useless, except for making the pouch to hold the rock.

Soon, weapon-making became the obsession in our small group of unsupervised boys. We made spears from long, straight sticks, their tips carved to a point and hardened in a fire. Slings were fashioned from a small pouch for the rock and two strings. Like David in "David and Goliath," we could hurl sizable rocks by twirling the two strings, then letting one go at the precise time. Mom's old nylon stockings could be loaded with stones and flung similarly, the hose becoming a long streamer on the way to the target.

Everything changed when we got our guns: a cocking or pump version of the Daisy B-B gun. B-Bs were cheap, even for a boy, and the range and nature of targets we could pursue moved to small animals, primarily birds. Although the memory fills me with disgust, I still remember a small bird falling like a stone from a twenty-foot-high tree branch and the "plop" sound when it hit the ground. A few years later, rats at the town dump scurried as they tried to avoid our 22 rifle bullets. We now have "real" guns, and everyone, even our parents, believed killing as many rats as possible was good.

The town dump was simply a place where garbage was taken and dumped. No bulldozer was used to cover it with dirt; it just piled there in a small mountain that grew by the day. Aside from a place to kill rats and spending much time there (our "playground"), we realized it was a treasure trove of valuable items to be sorted and set aside to be hauled home in our wagons. Even today, the idea of something free fills me with pleasure. Making something from almost nothing by investing my time and skills would influence me for the rest of my life. In my late fifties, I set on a journey to build my airplane.

The "loot" from the dump fell into various categories. Some items had no immediate use but were just too good not to take home. Some things had an immediate use but were in some disrepair and were taken home to be worked on. A broad category was anything that would help us build and furnish a shack in the woods. It started with building materials, mostly cardboard, and progressed to furnishings and even reading materials—old Life magazines. The shack forever drooped and disintegrated from the rain without a proper roof (a plastic sheet or canvas). The aroma of wet cardboard and old magazines wafted around our heads as we huddled in the shack after a summer rainstorm.

Summers were also a time to hang out at the river and, sometimes, a place we called the "lock wall." It was where the boats just emerged from or entered the lock to be raised or lowered the seven-foot height of the dam. We were a few feet from the towboat, a sternwheeler in the early years, or what some may call a paddleboat. We swam dangerously close to powerful eddies and were at risk of being crushed against the lock wall, but the knowledge of how to do such things was passed from older boys to younger boys by their example.

We also taught ourselves to swim. It was not a proper Australian crawl but a river swim with our heads held out of the water, our bodies turning side to side. Driven out of necessity, we had to be alert for sewage dumped in the river upstream of our town. We coined the Monongahela river "white fish" to describe the occasional condom that would float by.

The inevitable day was an essential right of passage; with no adult around, we swam across the river and back. Dares were never given because we knew that anyone who didn't make it would be lost in the mirky river, our parents throwing bread on the water to discover where the currents had taken the body. Safer dares, but beyond my nerve, were jumping off the lock wall into a barge of granulated coal, then running up the river on the barges, keeping stationary with friends on the shore, or swimming to the middle of the river and into the "wheelers," the turbulent water behind the sternwheeler's paddles. Later in the day, home for supper, no mention was made of where we had been or what risks we had taken. And no questions were asked by our parents.

Growing up on our own and without influence from the outside world or adults, we developed a code of conduct. It could be not kind regarding animals, yet surprisingly compassionate. When a stray dog showed up at the school playground, severely injured, one boy brought his gun to school and hid it in the woods so we could put the animal out of its misery. That was the sixth grade.

The years passed, and as we grew older, our attention turned to girls, and the days of weapon-making and building forts in the woods ended. We began to go our way without mentioning what we would do as adults. I was the exception, with a mom who said I should attend college. The other boys had no such expectations set upon them. They would graduate high school, marry, and live like their parents. In those days of hope, none of us knew that the mills would soon close, the unions would lose their power, and life would be forever changed, except for me; a college education would provide me with economic security for the rest of my life.

CHAPTER 30

TRUMAN SHOW IN MY RETIREMENT COMMUNITY

In the 1998 movie, "The Truman Show," Jim Carey stars as a man living in a television studio world. He doesn't know it—it's all so real—until it begins to fray at the edges. Unexpected reveals, endless repetitions of the familiar, and a wife whose wifely duties increasingly take her off-script.

Real life has tragedy, pain, and sometimes, not "Disney" perfect moments. Not for Truman. Millions of viewers hang on to his every mundane decision. It's a life like mine, but without the audience, here at The Villages, an over 55 retirement community in south-east San Jose, California.

A fence and a phalanx of safety patrol guards protect me from the outside world. It is high in the hills, above the pollution, crime, and hmmm of the lives of real people who work, have babies, and struggle to keep up their lawns. Golf carts and walking trails usher smiling faces from venue to venue, from swimming pool to a bocce court, and then to the Bistro for drinks, bad-for-you food, and inane conversation ... about golf, the next village event, or the best doctor for hip surgery.

Hundreds of "extras" mow the grass, groom the golf course, and dress the set for this picture-perfect world. One day blends into another, distinguished only by the Village newspaper's headline: movie night at the Vineyard Center, "John Wayne in "Paint Your Wagon," a prime rib from a serving cart with your choice of two extras, or a meeting of the ukulele club in the Sequoia Room.

The bucolic serenity is not interrupted by a silent fire truck and ambulance climbing the hills to retrieve the next victim of old age, poor genes, bad diet, or simply running out of time. An estate sale will soon be conducted to erase any evidence of their departure. Like the course gains in a salt shaker, the good stuff will stay, find a new home, and give the rest to GoodWill.

"Life" auditioned me for the Truman movie. Years of fighting Silicon Valley traffic, endless days in windowless cubicles, and finally concluding that my generation has lost its relevance. No one remembers Howdy Doodie and rotary dial telephones. So I drive to the front gate of The Villages. A visitor, soon to be a resident with a bar-coded entry sticker on my car, I find a newly vacant, sensible, one-story condo and enter a world of child-like irresponsibility. "Life is Short" becomes a battle cry from living every damn minute having fun, discarding concerns about global warming, a lying moron for a president, or the threat of nuclear war in the middle east. There is nothing I can do. It's that simple. Except ... the voter polling place is just out the gate, voting will be my last vestige of responsibility to leave behind a better world.

New residents are handed a road map to all the village attractions. It's like a map of Disneyland. The Bistro and the Clubhouse "concession," the wood shop, the auditorium, and the 18-hole golf course are noted. And buried in the back of my three-ring binder are guides to resources I may need. Healthy living, exercise, estate planning. Those pages will remain largely unturned.

I didn't join this "Truman" world to get fit, become a vegan, reduce my carbon footprint, or add two more months to my lifespan. I'm here to have fun and be happy, like Truman.

It's early morning, and driving in my golf cart to the nearest hot tub, I wave and smile at the dog walkers with their poop bags ready. "Have a great day!" They smile and return my greeting, turn a bend, and beyond my sight, a dog handler puts their dog in a carrier; they board a minivan to their next assignment: the Bistro patio.

CHAPTER 31

WHEELS ON MY SHOES, GROWING UP IN A SMALL TOWN

In my best imitation of an Olympic skater's crouch, my left arm aerodynamically tucked behind my back, my right arm swinging pendulum style to the stroke, the stroke of my skating. Dogs bark and strain at their leash. Children point and stare at the man with wheels on his shoes. Parents watch, reminded of their unused in-line skates in the hall closet — that halfway house of abandoned intentions on their way to a cousin or The Good Will. Grandparents and folks with a touch of grey in their hair also stare and smile. They are flooded with memories of sidewalk skating with clamp-on skates, wondering whatever happened to the skate key tied around their neck with a shoestring.

My roller skating is the only survivor from my 1950s childhood in Western Pennsylvania. The BB gun, my sister's bike, trips to the city dump, a reputation of a boy "looking for trouble," and, yes, my incredible freedom were all gone.

My two older sisters discovered roller skating long before I did. They learned how to skate-dance with a partner, sometimes another girl who could skate the boy's way, whirling around the rink to the two-step, the waltz, and something called the "Blues." By some miracle worked with the family finances; they had "precision skates." The sealed ball bearings and wooden wheels gave their skates an eerie silence as they turned and swooped, first into the center, then precariously close to the wall.

I learned to skate on the hilly and cracked sidewalks and quickly transitioned to the magnificent wooden floor of the roller skating rink at the end of town. Twenty-five cents bought four hours of skating to organ music from 12 inches 78's, and for my mom, four hours of freedom from my bleating that I had "nothing to do."

I leaned on the railing, waiting for the too-long organ music to stop and the announcement of "all-skate." There was nothing precise about my skating. My fiber wheels and loose ball-bearing skates were built for one thing: speed. I joined the other boys and rushed onto the floor, merging into and enveloped by the whirling mass of skaters. The young man with the whistle and the authority to have me sit this one out stared suspiciously.

I had to leave the floor when it was "couples-only." Girls could do it, but boys could never link hands and synchronize their skate-over-skate movements around the bends. It was the roller skating version of the Dutch children ice-skating on frozen canals. Whatever was lurking inside of me, that would have me walking for miles to pass a girl's house accidentally in two years, was still sleeping. I wanted no part of it, no couples skating.

While we were eating Saturday supper, the rink was being transformed into the town Bingo Hall. It was simple: long tables joined end to end were arranged in three rows on the skating floor. The organ music speakers became the voice of the bingo caller, perched on a balcony above the floor.

In that small town, we all gambled. As kids, we sat unrestrained in the back seat of mom's Packard car, our parent's gambling we would not fly through the window in a crash. No lifeguard was supervising the first time we swan across the Monongahela River to the other side, looking upriver, then down, for an approaching stern-wheeler riverboat. No helmet could be bought to protect our heads in a bike fall.

The men gambled with their lives. With his carbide lamp, the coal miner led the mine ponies into the underground darkness, hoping the timbers would hold. The steel worker, hoping that fate would not mingle his body with the ingot of molten steel. The river worker, hoping that a small slip would not plunge him into the river, his wife and relatives throwing slices of bread on the water to see where the currents had taken his body.

The women gambled with household money, small amounts, looking for a significant return for their circumscribed lives. My first exposure to this gambling ritual occurred at Christy's Candy Store. My mother waited for 25 cents, the equivalent of five ice cream cones, while Mr. Christy used a metal probe to push the small paper roll from its cell on the board. Mostly it said: "sorry, try again." Mom and her relatives played the "numbers" in hushed tones on the telephone. Great Aunt Goldie found her husband's life savings in rolls of cash in a cigar box; he could never trust a bank with that wealth. She carefully unwound the layers of money and made monthly jaunts to the Wheeling, West Virginia, horse track.

On Saturday night, hopes for a big Bingo winning were high, but it was also a social event for the woman. No husbands in sight — the men were off to the Elks, the Moose, or the Veterans of Foreign Wars (VFW). Memories of the War were still strong, but the specifics were rarely discussed. Their shared experiences drew them together to drink and walk side by side in the Memorial Day parade in front of the fire trucks from Harmony, Elizabeth, or Beaver Falls. Not my father; he wasn't accepted. He spent the war in the Merchant Marine, getting good pay, but not a real soldier.

I watched while my mother's accountant mind managed eight Bingo cards, dropping kernels of corn on the numbers like a human planting machine. Sometimes her mother, known to me by the country name "Me-maw," with her purchased translucent red tokens, would join her. Every game followed the same ritual: the first 7-8 numbers rarely spawned a Bingo. As the following number was called, side conversations, comments about lousy luck, and laughter gave way to silence.

Then there was a pause as we waited for an explosive "Bingo" to split the air or, as moments passed, to feel the exhilaration of still being in the game.

Bingo's winnings were five to ten dollars, and in the case of multiple Bingos, split between the winners. On the other hand, the jackpot Bingo, at twenty-five to fifty dollars, could open up possibilities. For my mom, it meant extra grocery money, a few cartons of Chesterfield cigarettes as proffered by Arthur Geoffrey — the smoke we would breathe in our closed-up winter house, or a trip to Dr. Stoller, the town doctor, for a shot of Vitamin B-12. My mother would sit in the waiting room of his house office for the image that would, for a while, put a smile on her face and a spring in her step. In our town, it was the drug for sad-faced ladies after opiates, like Laudanum, and before modern anti-depressants, like Prozac, were developed.

When we moved from the town to the country, a long four miles, I put my roller skates away and would not skate again for forty years. I entered a different world seemingly devoid of adults, where I joined the other boys to live a life of complete freedom. The boundaries were as far as we could walk and still get home in time for supper. Our domain included Lock Number Three on the Monongahela river, the abandoned coal mine with its dark mouth beckoning for exploration, the grape and fruit orchards left for wild, and best of all, the smoldering city dump.

Our only dependency on adults was for the ten dollars to purchase a BB gun and necessary equipment. Not even the fear of blindness from a stray BB could sway mom from the opportunity to get me out of the house to join the other boys, Hixie, Ben, and Chucky, all fully armed.

We shot anything that moved – birds, rats, stray cats – and some things that didn't move but had the bad fortune to look like a target: street lights, stop signs. As the sons of mill workers and river people, our dads and relatives taught us by their example that it was okay to kill animals or birds. It was never about hunger or survival, it was about dominance, and there was an inexhaustible supply of things to kill. Our BB gun was preparing us for the twenty-two, the shotgun, then the rifle and the opportunity to kill a deer and proudly drive through town (a few times) with it roped to the hood. I now look back at this killing with disgust, remembering how that perfect shot with a BB smaller than a pea could strike a bird and have it fall like a stone and that terrible sound when it hit the ground.

But the BB gun was not our only weapon. With a gun leaning against a tree, we made slingshots and rubber band guns from stripes of rubber cut from inner car tubes. We made spears, and when our building skills improved, we bows and arrows. A rock in the bottom of mom's nylon stocking became a sling. We picked up stones and threw them when there was nothing left to shoot or sling.

And then there was the Fourth of July. The ad in the back of the comic book was barely large enough on which to write your name and address. You could have the "Battle of the Bulge" fireworks sent to your home for five dollars. The Banner Fireworks Company was somewhere in Ohio, and after a begging session with mom for the money, I waited for the box to arrive at the Railway Express Station and farm feed store at the side of the railroad tracks in town.

No Army general was more pleased than I was as I opened the box and sorted the munitions for the upcoming day of destruction. Cherry bombs and Tanks were counted and reserved for huge targets. The smaller firecrackers were unwoven for one-by-one small explosions. Ladyfingers were useless and given to my sister. We spent the day roaming the neighborhood looking for anything to blow up. It could be an empty soup can or something as serious as a mailbox. Nothing escaped our carnage as punk after punk burned down. The smell of gunpowder filled the air the entire day and into the night. The next day the "duds" were collected and taken apart for the gunpowder and the opportunity for bomb-making. We learned that firecrackers were made from newspaper and gunpowder, rolled very tightly, and then covered with tissue. The watermelon picture on the package suggested they were made somewhere far away, like Louisiana or China.

Now approaching our teen years, we realized that our BB guns were no match for the rats at the city dump, so we moved on to more firepower: twenty-two rifles. Everyone agreed, even our parents, that reducing the rat population was good. Spending more and more time at the dump, the shooting gave way to scavenging for building materials or anything so good it was a crime to throw away. It was today's Wall Mart with everything marked down to zero. We were lucky.

Orange crates, cardboard, and discarded building materials were carried, dragged, and hauled on wagons to our shack deep in the woods. It was a place to smoke mom's Chesterfields, read old Life magazines, or build a fire to roast potatoes. I still can remember the smell of wet cardboard and damp books. We never discussed the future or any event more distant than starting school in the fall.

As summer after summer passed, and as we shot and exploded things around our neighborhood, a kid's code of ethics evolved. It was okay to throw mud balls at passing cars if they did not have a rock buried in the center. It was okay to tip over to the school bus shelter if no adults could see you — it didn't hurt anything. It was okay to shoot animals, especially wild animals, but it was never okay to shoot a dog. There was one exception.

We attended a three-room school — each room having three grades. The large rooms had a coal stove, and a cloakroom used to make ink and run ditto copies. I was in the classroom for sixth, seventh, and eighth grade. I practiced penmanship using the Peterson Method with a quill pen dipped in ink well at my desk while the teacher taught various subjects to the kids in seventh and eighth grades.

As bigger boys, we dominated the playground, scaring and teasing the girls with crawfish plucked from the creek near the school. One day a dog appeared at the edge of the garden and caught our attention. It was severely injured, had open wounds, and could barely walk. We shared our sandwiches with the dog, thinking we could make it well with that nourishment. As the days went by, it became apparent that our dog would not get well. Something had to be done. In our world, telling the teacher or a parent never occurred. No one had ever heard the word "veterinarian."

We decided it had to be shot to put it out of its misery; there was no other way — like a horse with a broken leg. A boy called Buckwheat carried his rifle to school, hiding it in the woods near the school. At lunch, we lured the barely walking dog deeper into the woods, fed it our sandwiches as a last meal, said good-by, and shot it.

It was the right thing to do, but I never told anyone, not my mother, college friends, or wife. Many years later, at work, I told this story to best someone who was describing his wild boyhood. But there was no laughing; everyone stared at me in disbelief.

Like the farmer who lifts the calf every day in hopes of someday lifting a cow, I imagine I can outrun my mortality, that shadowy figure that hangs out at hospitals and nursing homes, someone I occasionally see in the mirror of my skate helmet. I needed more speed.

Help came from Frank, who lives in Philadelphia. He owns a roller-skating rink and skates supply business. I found him on the Internet after discovering that Google believes I have "quads," not roller skates. I didn't order online; I called Frank to talk things over. He reminded me of Mr. Gondoli, that big man behind the counter at the roller rink of my childhood. He said, "You need a complete overhaul: truck bushings, grommets, wheels, bearings, and toe stops."

The parts came neatly sealed in plastic bags. I rebuilt the trucks, mounted the translucent red Kyptonic 70 mm polyurethane wheels and Red Bones sealed ball bearings, and went for a test run.

My skating has brought me full circle from growing up in a small town. Almost everything has changed — growing up with a gun and trips to the city dump is forever lost to this generation, yet one thing still survives. And thanks to Frank, I have more speed.

"On your left."

CHAPTER 32

COLLECTION: LOVE AND LOVING

CHAPTER 33

CAT LOVE

It's 6:30 AM. I'm drinking my first 1/2 cup of coffee, lost in thought. Angelo gives me a head butt; he wants to make love. I'm a morning person, but now? OK, I scratch his neck as he sits in my lap. It's nothing kinky, just two guys in love. Later, he raises his head, and we exchange a long glance. He runs to his food bowl; I sigh and reach for an imaginary cigarette.

CHAPTER 34

CLAIRE'S WORLD

Claire's arms are outstretched as if to hug me, and she is laughing, with a toothy expression and glimmer in her eyes that signals my invitation to enter her world. She is on her back, on the rug, where she spends most of her life. My memory and most of the photographs will always place her there. Almost five, her tiny body would confuse a stranger who might at first turn away and later ask, "Is she two; does she have Down's Syndrome?"

Claire has a genetic disease called I-cell. It has a long medical name, Mucolipidosis II, that I seldom mention in my practiced explanation of her condition. Most people on this planet, even doctors, will live their entire life and never hear the term "I-cell." And by some mysterious turning and twisting of the DNA pathways and their improbable alignment, Claire is a child we are constantly saying goodbye to. I say it with a twinge of guilt because my DNA is a part of the "gear alignment" that put her on the floor, never to walk or grow into a girl, a woman.

I leave these thoughts behind for a moment and move closer to her. She waits for me to say something. "Claire, do you want to play?" She knows the cadence of a question and will always answer, "yea." Sometimes I hear a fragment from the song "Old McDonald has a farm..." Her world is not spoken words; it's a rich vocabulary of gestures, laughs, smiles, and body movements. When Claire says, "no," I don't need the word. She is done with her food or a toy that she dislikes. Language is not just words; communication is more than two people talking to each other. I find a tiny cup and start drinking "tea."

Claire likes to pretend, as all children do, and we constantly pretend that we have an important job, like filling a container with small game parts, the head of a lego character, arms and legs, and small amounts of plastic fruit. Her role is to empty the container, which she does with relish, flinging the contents as widely as she can. Of course, we do it again and again and again.

One of Claire's favorite "pretend" is talking on the phone. It can be a small block of plastic—it's not essential—the conversation continues for minutes. I listen to her chatter, the pauses, the responses to an imaginary voice, and try to match a single word, but I can't. Somehow, though, Claire is talking with *her* words, and I do not doubt that she thinks so too.

If you imagine that I-cell makes Claire a passive, unresponsive little girl, you're mistaken. She is as willful and aggressive as her brothers and sister, and she is keenly aware of what they are doing and wants to be part of it. I admire her spirit and the fact that she is fighting to be in their world and be one of the family. Claire's passing will leave a hole as wide or wider than any "normal" child you will ever see. There is no moving to the back of the line; she will fight for her place in the family as long as she is with us.

I say goodbye. I say it repeatedly, and I see she knows what it means.

I will return to say goodbye for as long as I can.

CHAPTER 35

ONE FINAL WORD ABOUT LOVE

Everything we need to know about love has been written, captured in song, embossed in poetry, spoken from the altar, whispered in dark rooms, or iconized in cupid drawings of lovestruck men, obviously out of their minds. It's one of the early words we hear in the crib and then put away for the day when we meet that particular person. It has more shades of meaning than any other word and is further nuanced by when and how it is said and, sometimes, how often. You can love spaghetti or the color of your new car, but the stakes are suddenly higher when it's a person you love.

"I love you, grandmother" can be safely said without qualification or any further need for clarification. No one puzzles a deeper intent or hidden agenda; grandmother's love is as pure as it gets. But from there, saying" I love you" gets increasingly risky, and one needs to ensure a proper context where such expressions are understood.

For example, loving a friend of the same sex is rarely expressed, especially for men. Circumscribing the boundaries of such love must be done so carefully that it inevitably tarnishes the purity of the feeling. And yet, unspoken or not, we have seen many examples of men who love each other, especially in war. From that, we conclude that love can blossom and live in areas of our lives that have nothing to do with gender or desire for physical intimacy.

Nevertheless, the same word, when spoken to a person of the opposite sex, runs such a wide gambit of meaning that it could lead to the bedroom or a comment on a birthday card for someone you have known since childhood. It's a failure of our language that we don't have different words to make such distinctions. Instead, we either refrain from saying it or take on an inordinate effort to frame the proper intent. And saying it too often or at the wrong time could unintentionally cause it to leap like a spark from the greeting card to the bedroom. Often, we include the excellent relationship, like "friend," with the word to coral the intended meaning.

And when the gloves are off, and we are in love (emphasis on the word "in"), it's not a qualification we want, but a stronger word to describe how we feel. All the other "loves" seem to dilute the more profound and intensely felt emotion. And so, lacking another love word, we tail adjectives to the word, even though "fully," "deeply," and words like that imply a physical description of something more spiritual.

The most exciting aspect of a profession of love is when the dimensions and perimeter need to be better defined. This lack of precision of the word creates a mirky space where emotions and feelings need to be explored and agreed upon. Elizabeth Browning did so in her poem, "Sonnets from the Portuguese," with the lines, "I love thee to the depth and breadth and height. My soul can reach."

Sometimes it's not words but actions that build the house of many rooms. For love to endure, it needs to be furnished and attended to. If not, love has a way of fading, even disappearing. It's not so much a destination (to be loved) as it describes a journey (loving).

Unrequited love might be the most painful and tragic of the "loves" when there is something far worse. Unrequited love is well-defined and something that eventually must be accepted. What is worse is when two people feel the stirrings of love, but distance or circumstance makes it impossible for it to grow. It's the beautiful highway with no on-ramp, the pile of combustibles with no oxygen. The impossibility of the situation stunts all the imagined fulfillment, and there is no way the gap can be bridged. It lives a half-life of new feelings, nourished by a hug, a glance that is held beyond propriety, a kiss on the cheek, or shared words of intimacy that cross the line of simple friendship. Having no "legs," it remains the hole in the heart never filled, the promise never delivered upon.

What is the final word about love? My experience has made me believe it is the two words "leaning toward." The root of all love is the physical, spiritual, and psychological act of leaning toward someone who is loved. It's the inclination and direction that moves a person to enter a bonding with another person. The expression and the exploration of what follows will take one of the many paths I have mentioned above. It will be beautiful, and it may be painful, and it will inevitably define who you are as a human being.

CHAPTER 36

HAROLD ALBERT WATSON

Harold Albert "DOC" Watson, my father, was never a doctor. He was given that nickname as a young man when he served in the Navy. That was before he met my mother and before the smile and hopeful expectation departed his face from family photographs. I think he could have been a doctor or some other professional man, someone who wore a white shirt and tie, but that expectation and the low ceiling of the hard-working people of that generation and that part of country-western Pennsylvania - made that a un dreamable possibility.

He was a shadowy figure that was in and out - mostly out - of my childhood experience. Early in his marriage, and by working away on the rivers and oceans, he abdicated his role as a family leader. He became an occasional guest in our home. My mom filled the void, and I grew up in a matriarchal household with three sisters and no role model of what a man should be. I looked to my cousins and uncles, but I saw the externals: buying beer by the case, fixing your car, and holding down a mill job... if you were lucky. Their family life was behind closed doors; I could only imagine what that would be.

My mom was angry at what fait and her early immaturity had bestowed upon her, and I was influenced by the idea that a man was not to be trusted and might neglect his family in unforgivable ways. There was always a paycheck and a good one by the standards of the time, but not a man who would share the duties and responsibilities of running a family.

And he was not there to play ball with me or take me to "something"? Or go hunting, fix the family car, or paint the house. There was time for that between his away times; though he never took up the mantle of fatherhood, that was never to happen. I wonder if it was missing from his childhood - a doting mother, a father who threw him out of the house at an early age. Making his way as a lone figure, never in a family context, he may lack any better example of being a father.

I remember how he showed his love and pride in me in less obvious ways. I had never heard the words "I love you" in my whole life. He belonged to a generation of parents who didn't spoil their kids with such expressions. Love was demonstrated by providing food and shelter and the discipline to bend the flight of the child's arrow in the right direction.

He answered my incessant question of "why daddy" and encouraged me to pull my shoulders back (my failure at that is visible today). He brought exotic toys from distant ports of call - a scooter from Holland. A Lionel train and an erector set with an electric motor descended at times when he returned home from an extended absence.

Each time he carried home his tools from the engine rooms of boats and ships that bore his initials, stamped into the metal with a set of lettered chisels, "H A W." They were the physical manifestation of his identity and value as a man. Someday, he would frequently say, later in life, "when I am gone, I want you to have these."

I still have some of the tools. I used some to build an airplane. And I have his admonitions in my mind as I stand in front of a mirror and realize I need to pull my shoulders back. And I know that he truly loved me and never, for a moment, abdicated his responsibilities to the family and me. If he were here today, I would tell him that I loved him and forgive him for never playing ball with me or those other measures we impose on dads. He did the best he could. I know that.

CHAPTER 37

HOW I SURVIVE

"How deep is the ocean?" "How high is the sky?"

Those early expressions of the unknowable capture our inability to understand love and love. Scientists have answered those worldly questions, but we still struggle to understand the importance of love in our lives.

Something we all agree upon. Everyone needs to love and be loved. The consequences of its absence are too undeniable to be ignored. Most benignly, its lack brings unhappiness and malaise. In extreme ways, it can lead to unfathomable consequences. It may be an oversimplification, but physiologists are prone to peel back the layers of a failed life and uncover the absence of love. Are they right?

In our early life, after we leave the loving envelope of our parents and family, we go out into the world and cast our net far and wide to find love. We may "throwback" love that doesn't meet our goals, and we are eager to continue to find love and don't stop the search. Our goal is to wrap ourselves in the glow of being loved and bask in the warmth of its embrace.

Marriage is designed to celebrate the "catch" and declare the search to be over for a lifetime. Sometimes that happens, and we hold up those examples to venerate or, more likely, to assume guilt when it doesn't happen. How can we hold onto a particular outcome in a decision that spans a lifetime, made at an early age, and fought with so many exigencies? But we do.

All this uncertainty begs the question: how do we survive the loss of love, especially in the late years of our lives? Given the innate desire to be loved that never goes away, what can we do to find a modicum of happiness? The answer, for some, comes full circle from our childhood ... when we felt alone and wanted a friend to share our every childhood dream with, we invented an imaginary friend. Always there, ready to have a conversation, and loving us without limit.

CHAPTER 38

A LOVE LETTER TO EMMA WATSON

From Grandpa, on her second birthday.

October 8, 2006

Dear Emma,

You have been with us for two years, and I love you more than ever. When I am with you, there is nothing else – the whole world stops and circles your countenance.

When I am with you, I sometimes weep. I weep because you are so beautiful. It's hard not to turn away from such physical beauty. It pulls at something in me I can't describe. I weep because you are so beautiful in every other way – a child who hugs and says "OK," laughs, and dances for the slightest reason.

I weep because the world is not beautiful enough for you; it should be better and happier. I felt the same way about your father thirty-some years ago.

I want to roll a magic carpet in front of you. It would lead you to beauty and discovery and have only enough bumps to prepare you for the world, but no dead ends, missed opportunities and pain.

Run Emma. Run with your arms open. Be a girl, teenager, young woman, or whatever you want. I want to live forever so I can be there at every step, waiting to catch you if you fall, ready to cheer every accomplishment and celebrate your beautiful life.

Love,
Pa-Pa Watson

CHAPTER 39

NEVER LOVED A PEACH?

If you don't love a peach floating in brown sugar and cream
You've never touched a woman's breast.
Or kneaded dough for bread
You've never flirted to the edge of infidelity.
Then pulled back, basking in the sweetness of what could have been,
Or held the hand of your granddaughter on a walk to nowhere,
Or take your firstborn in your arms and stare into infinity.
Eating peaches is no sin, the calories forgotten,
It's the door to transcendence.
A gift from our primordial soup.

CHAPTER 40

DO I LOVE OR HATE MY BODY?

We have a love-hate relationship with our bodies, and it's not the mirror returning a less-than-Hollywood-perfect image, although, for many, that may be reason enough. No, it's the failures of our flesh that, mistakenly, seem to be entirely out of our control. We love a body that can swim a length in the pool, ride a bicycle, or respond to a lover's caress, but we hate the body that pauses in a flight of stairs, sags, and droops beyond concealment, or worse, and for no apparent reason, gets ill. We curse the imperfect vessel that weakly transports our brains around the planet and delivers our souls too soon to heaven.

It's not always that way. Children represent the complete fusion of mind and body. A child will skip and leap for no apparent reason in a celebration of mind and body that has no separation. We start our journey in life with that perfect harmony, and yet, somewhere along the way, we begin to live more in mind and less in the body. The body, being the wonderful instrument it is, cooperates with this priority and delivers everything the mind wants with little complaint.

It does that beyond reason, and for as long as it can until one day, it delivers less than we want, and we are disappointed. Strangely, we are surprised by this failure and may even feel anger or hate toward it. We search for answers to reinforce the idea that we are the innocent victim of a flawed body. Was it our family genes, a childhood fall at the skating rink, a spray of toxic fumes as we walked by an industrial plant, or bad luck?

In a moment of self-honesty, we may also ask: was it neglect, of not paying attention to its health, that is to blame? Have I been a good body-Stewart? It's an opportunity for reflection on what we have been eating and drinking, what exercise we have elected to do or not, and whether we have listened to the small signals the body delivers after a period of excess or neglect.

What does a mind know about a body? Sadly, the answer is often less than necessary to lead a long and healthy life. Our cultural model of the body, especially in the United States, is that of a motorcar. It needs fuel and occasional maintenance but little else. It can be driven as much as you want and never needs rest time in the garage. Ironically, we may know more about caring for our cars than our bodies.

Unless educated, the mind has no concern for the quality or purity of our food or the value of exercise and good sleep. There is little reinforcement for these ideas in mainstream American life. And religion, for the most part, views the body as an imperfect vessel for the soul. We are encouraged to love God, but in an unspoken way, discouraged from the sin of worshiping our bodies by paying attention to worldly things such as nutrition and exercise. Is it "worshipping" or honoring and respecting the body? We are left to decide that question on our own.

"Health nuts" at the fringes of society advocate blenderized concoctions of raw vegetables as the proper diet. Deeply sculptured men or woman mount stone age-looking medieval torture instruments for exercise. It's easy to tune them out. As for training, sports have been co-opted by professional athletes on television screens that we watch passively from our couches. We could never do that. Looking for an easy solution to our body issues, we turn to the pharmaceutical industry for a pill that will reduce blood pressure, lower cholesterol, take off unwanted pounds, and even produce an erection should we get in the mood for sex.

The journey back to the child-like love of the body is none of the above. There is no formula to be followed. Like so many things in life, it starts with the knowledge that the body, not just the mind, needs to be fed good food. It also begins with an act of faith that the reward for the journey back to mind and body health will be more joyful than anyone can fully articulate. The rest of the story—what to eat, how to exercise—will unfold before you.

CHAPTER 41

MY MOTHER, THE VAMP

After viewing an old family photo.

I never thought of my mom as a vamp. But here she is, looking vampish. I want to imagine her early life was carefree, and she was a young woman with hope and promise. What happened?

Along the way, it became a sad life, full of anger and regrets. I, her only son, became the man she never had in her life, never married, someone with class, intelligence, and a "man who would wear a tie," like her distant and enigmatic father. I didn't know it then, but it was a heavy burden for a boy. I did my best to meet her expectations, attending a "rich-kid" military school and getting good grades.

The sacrifices she made and the whole family made for me to do that are a staggering and bitter-sweet memory. I hope she had moments, maybe between her many heart attacks, where she felt happy and contented sitting with a TAB and a cigarette. Maybe for just a moment - that would be enough - for me to view her life as something more than tragedy.

A long shout across the passage of time... "I love you, mom. Thanks."

CHAPTER 42

COLLECTION: TRANSCENDENCE

CHAPTER 43

FLYING HIGH

Is this plane a silver coffin or a beautiful spaceship? It doesn't matter; I'm too needy to calculate living or dying. I'm desperate to leave my earth-bound life and climb up and away from my prison world where gravity and people hold me in bondage.

I settle back, my seat tray still upright and locked, and wait for the rarified air to transport me to that transcendent place between heaven and earth. The San Francisco Bay is already slipping away as the morning sun arcs across the wing and passes out of sight. The 160 people around me are strangers and have no pull on me. And I have escaped the grasp of the people below—all those needy hands that tie me down.

My body is unaware of the speed as I race across the Sierra mountains and onto the western plains on my way to North Carolina. I have no physical feeling as my mind separates from my body and suspends above the plane, the veils of earthly concern and confusion falling away.

A fundamental truth about my life is suddenly clear. I now understand why I'm here and how I should live. Why didn't I see it before? It's so simple. What I thought was important is now inconsequential. The chaff falls away, and the key to living and being happy is before me. Everything will be different when I land, step out of the plane, and start my new life. Every second will be precious.

Satisfied with my enlightenment, I look out the window at my feathery bed beneath the white clouds beneath me. Nothing wrong can happen. I could fall into their soft arms and be saved. A euphoric feeling of well-being envelops me.

Time passes, and soon, my revelry is interrupted by a distant voice. It's the pilot. We're going to begin our descent into Charlotte. Looking out the window, I see the ground and then familiar landmarks. The red earth reminds me of my first trip here and how strange it looked. I'm continually amazed that anything grows, but it's lush, verdant, and inviting to me.

My sister and brother-in-law will be picking me up. It will be great to see them again and have two weeks of cutting firewood and doing farm projects.

The bright North Carolina landscape surprises me when I emerge from the terminal. I could be blindfolded and dropped off here, and I would know right away. It's North Carolina!

My sister asks me about the flight. I have to pause a moment before answering.

"Yes," I say, "it was uneventful—a smooth flight."

The car accelerates away from the airport, and I have a vague feeling that I have forgotten something. It doesn't matter; I can buy a forgotten item in town.

CHAPTER 44

GREEN CURRY AND RICE

Giggling and teasing one another in a language I didn't understand, the five young Thai women went about their chores to ready the restaurant for dinner. A young male manager shouted something, his staccato voice echoing off the bare walls, their laughter erupting and ricocheting from one to another until they all laughed and touched each other playfully.

They looked similar to my western eye, yet each wore a necklace, a piece of hair jewelry, or a belt to transform their black waitress uniforms into a distinctive costumes. Their black hair, deep-red lipstick, and Asian-slender bodies gave them an air of the exotic, like mistresses in a movie about American soldiers in Vietnam.

It was a choreography of their familiar and mindless tasks, like a ballet, stacking the take-out containers, replenishing the pile of chopsticks, and filling the water glasses for the expected crush of diners. With customers rapidly filling the restaurant, they finished their chores without pausing or speaking, then moved to assigned positions.

The silver necklace waitress approached my table, stopped abruptly, and looked so directly at me that, for a moment, I wasn't sure why I was there or what to say. In our polite society, especially between a man and woman, holding a glance that long is not permitted, but there she was, not avoiding my eyes and waiting for my response.

I blurted, "A beer, yes, I'll have a beer, A Kiren beer, a draft Kiren beer…"

I was unconsciously adding more and more qualifications in an attempt to make the moment last. Ordering the meal could take a long time, but before I could choose the variety and size of the rice and whether I wanted chopsticks or a fork, she was gone, leaving me staring at the residual image of her my mind had constructed and was unwilling to let go of.

The beer appeared, soon becoming another fixture in the frozen moment. Her eyes were the only life in an otherwise enigmatic expression. I couldn't think about ordering. Food rapidly descended to the bottom of my "Maslowian" pyramid of needs.

I hesitated, then spoke, "No, I want to order later," my finger traveling down the side of the glass like a sight gauge, indicating when I wanted her to return.

The alcohol was soon racing in my head, and I felt dizzy and transcendent. I have never known a Thai person, dated one, or had a conversation longer than today. I had no frame of reference to build an imaginary conversation, construct an overture that would lead to a date, or take her hand and walk out of the restaurant. I could only think of the movie, "The Silent American," and imagine I was Michael Cane and the young Vietnamese woman was Thai. I could see her carefully preparing my opium pipe and making me comfortable; the air in the restaurant was suddenly fecund and heavy with expected pleasure.

The room was filling quickly, and soon the silver necklace returned to my table. I recited my order while she silently nodded.

A smile crossed her face when she said, "Green Curry and rice. Thank you."

"No," I said, looking at her directly, "Thank you."

CHAPTER 45

FINDING TRANSCENDENCE AT 30K FEET

I'm a belted prisoner in this aluminum tube, suspended in time, captive in an unwanted intimacy with 150 strangers, and forced to believe that two more strangers in the cockpit know how to get this plane to San Francisco and land. Nothing is a certainty in this life, not San Francisco, and not the destination for someone like me, someone who is falling. I'm giddy from lack of oxygen in this rarefied atmosphere, hoping for a moment of transcendence to show me the way.

Sperm and egg dance. It's not a courtship; there's no time; it's urgent. No time to ponder if this life is wanted or necessary. No time to examine the delicate strands of DNA for a defect, a bad connection to set in motion a heart attack at age 30. You aren't asked if you want to take this journey, to know if you are wanted. And soon, you're traveling that dark canal to cold and light, gasping for air and helpless.

Like the young wildebeest on the Serengeti, in no time, you're galloping alongside your mother for a destination not of your choosing. It's always been this way. We follow the trails laid down by those who came before us.

We search for maps, and there are none. The markers fly by, and we pause briefly to celebrate a birthday, graduation, or marriage; nothing has any lasting meaning. We're told the journey is the reward, and we look outside of ourselves, often mistaking motion for living.

We struggle to assign meaning to our lives and often allow others to do that for us. Success, happiness, and achievement are well-defined. We can live our whole life and achieve nothing that merits a celebration. And if it did, what would it mean?

Looking out the airplane's window this night, I see only specks of light from nameless towns populated with anonymous people. I'm up here, and they are down there, but aren't we all fellow travelers?

What if I knew the name of the town? What if I knew some of the people? What if I could look into their hearts and know their innermost secrets, hopes, dreams, and fears? We can choose to travel alone, or we can choose to travel with someone. We can walk alongside (like the people on this plane) or journey together with a deeper connection.

The plane will land soon, and I will walk away from these people, but when I return to my life, I will continue to choose the more profound connection. I've been on these roads for a long time, time enough the know that roads are not that important; fellow travelers are.

CHAPTER 46

COLLECTION: ECONOMICS

CHAPTER 47

BRADDOCK

Several years ago, Braddock, Pennsylvania, was the "poster child" of the new urban decay, a window into the economic upheaval brought on by first the loss of steel making in the nineteen eighties and then the out-sourcing of manufacturing jobs that dealt the final death blow to the descendants of eastern European immigrants who first settled the Monongahela valley in the eighteen seventies and found good laboring jobs. Braddock was to be a test case for urban renewal and re-birth. The young Harvard graduate mayor, John Fetterman, became a magnet for the media and photographers parking their rental cars in safe places. At the same time, they photographed the blight, the graffiti, the dark factories, and the boarded-up restaurants and shops. America was briefly interested. But they weren't there long enough to notice the beautiful buildings, the first Carnegie Library, the bank building, the churches—all in disrepair, and some hiding behind boarded-up doorways.

When they got back into their cars and drove back to the airport, and when UPMC closed the Braddock hospital in 2010, the two thousand residents of this town, a mere one-tenth of its former population, were left to struggle and try to find a footing without the glare of the media spotlight.

Today, the town's "victory" garden, a kind of urban greenery, is not as tidy as it appeared in the first photographs sent out. But there is hope. Some new housing—not a lot— is under construction. There are signs that the remaining commerce has "dug in" for the long haul, hoping to survive until some undefined better time arrives.

The ultimate fate of Braddock hangs in the balance. If there is any economic vitality in the region, and there is plenty in Pittsburgh, it's not beating a path to Braddock. It's too far from the city, and its resemblance to a war zone resists the crossing of its borders by the tentacles of urban gentrification.

Braddock is down on a gurney; the doctors have pulled back, and its proud citizens' gritty determination keeps it alive. My hometown, Elizabeth, only a few miles farther up the river, is also on a gurney. I wish them well. Our land of prosperity was built on the backs of these immigrants. , and they deserve a hand if only one can be found.

CHAPTER 48

JOBS AIN'T COMING BACK

"These jobs are going, boys, and they ain't coming back" ...

Bruce Springsteen penned that line about his hometown in the song "My Hometown." It was the closing of a textile mill that would never make today's news — they've been gone for years. And so have the steel mills, a large number of auto plants, the TV assembly plants, the machine shops, the silicon foundries, etc. The list is too long, and the point has already been made: we are no longer a manufacturing country. And so what? At first blush, it doesn't seem to matter; we've moved on unless it's personal unless you know someone whose manufacturing job "ain't coming back." Maybe it's an uncle in Pittsburgh, a former steel worker, who fills his days watching TV or hanging out with his buddies at a local bar. Across the country, people who once made a good wage are now Walmart greeters or flipping burgers and have no health benefits, collateral damage from the tectonic shift to cheaper labor, and the belief that just like the buggy whip maker, you will find another excellent job.

Now, as we look for signs that the recession is easing, the general expectation is that unemployment will drop as the economy recovers and new jobs are created. Prosperity will spread across the economic landscape like kudzu, and historians and op-ed writers will tell us why it happened and why it is thankfully over. For the unemployed scanning the want ads, the relevant question is: what specific job? Is it your old job, something you were trained for, or is it a job that takes you down the economic food chain toward minimum wage and no healthcare benefits? In the halls of Washington and the back rooms of economic think tanks, it will be concluded that it doesn't matter; it's recovery, pure and simple: a job is a job.

To examine what new jobs will be created and ones that won't, it is first necessary to look at a two-decade-long trend that has been underway, operating well below the national consciousness. Long before bundled mortgages, derivatives, and plain old greed decimated our economy, the slow and inexorable off-shore movement of our economic "treasure" was underway. Hard-won American technical know-how is sold cheaply to third-world countries in exchange for short-term market opportunities. China is learning how to make airplanes, thanks to joint ventures with Boeing. Chinese engineers, educated at our best universities, are back home designing our next computers and data storage systems (that they will manufacture). American companies are farming-out design work to China to save the cost of expensive Silicon Valley engineers. In India, software engineers are writing new code for our complex products. American managers are setting their alarm clocks to conference with their design teams in China and India.

Ironically, third-world countries that colonialist American and European companies once exploited for their natural resources are now "mining" our country for intellectual and technical knowledge in the form of reverse colonialism. Not surprisingly, there are people and corporations here promoting this type of export as an opportunity to gain a short-term but unsustainable advantage. It appears to be a win-win for everyone: industry, government, and stockholders. So, who loses?

It's not rocket science; the American worker loses. If this loss of livelihood were due to a natural disaster, forces would be mobilized, and our call to action would be loud, but it's not. It's a slow, town-by-town, city-by-city closing of the doors and turning off the lights, first in factories and now in engineering labs. Some economists would have you believe it's a healthy reallocation, re-direction of our economic strength. Other Google, Microsoft, Cisco, Apple, and NetApp will emerge to revitalize our economy and maintain our economic leadership. It may not happen. The cadre of qualified folks to do this re-inventing is diminishing by the day and will continue as more and more of our intellectual capital shifts to other countries.

The most telling indicator of gloom is a simple question posed to my co-workers, engineers, and scientists who entered the profession when it was a lifelong ticket to employment and prosperity. "Would you recommend a career in engineering and science for your son and daughter?" The answer was swift and unequivocal, "no." Can a country lead the economic parade without leadership in manufacturing and technology? An economist or politician is pondering that question and puzzling about how to say yes. That's what we want to hear.

CHAPTER 49

LAST ENGINEER STANDING

The last US engineer standing is a grey-haired, soon-to-be-retired person whose career spanned a time when products were designed and built in America. He has hand's-on experience in the product execution cycle from inception through manufacturing and delivery to the marketplace. He may have, for example, started his career at Zenith Radio in the fifties or sixties, when Zenith engineers designed radios, phonograph players, and televisions on the second floor and manufactured those products on the first floor of a large building in Chicago, Illinois. The building is still there, the roof parking lot littered with cars, the factory windows broken, and the name "Zenith," although remaining on the water tower, sold to a Korean company.

He has a well-used passport and can awaken at odd hours for conference calls with his design teams in China and India. Over the last several decades, his company has slowly thinned the ranks of engineers. Initially, the decline resulted from productivity improvements: Computer-Aided Design (CAD) systems, automated test equipment, and advances in product design methodology. As global competition intensified and the cost to employ a US engineer increased (salary, health care, company retirement contributions, and infrastructure costs), his management started looking outside the country. Not surprisingly, the engineers in foreign countries who had graduated from our best Universities and returned to their lands were competent and eager to use their skills. And they were cheaper. His company called it a "no-brainer" decision.

No one disputes the loss of US manufacturing. Several years ago, a newspaper columnist wrote about her attempt to live one day using only "Made in America" products. It's become so absurd that even the patriotic slogan "Buy American" has been abandoned. Across America, slowly at first and now at dizzying speed, the lights are being turned off at US factories. Initially, the number of layoffs in small cities — as in 2004, the 989 employees in a Marion, Ohio TV plant — were reported like battlefield causalities in an economic "war." Now it no longer makes the evening news. The total number of laid-off employees is a seldom reported but staggering figure. Like the death of soldiers in war, the impact on the families and their communities defies description.

The infrastructure for manufacturing: tool and die, makers, printed circuit manufacturing, silicon foundries, sheet metal fabricators, and so on, have also relocated abroad. Now our engineering capability is being replicated in those countries, aided by the export of our technology and our University training. The international students who graduate from our Universities are now staying in the country that educated them. They are being joined by many colleagues who initially stayed on but now find more significant opportunities by returning to their homelands.

Politicians promise the lights can be turned on again in those factories in an initiative to have the US become the leader in "Green" energy technology. Perhaps it can, but a closer look at the factories will find them empty. The manufacturing equipment has been auctioned off, on the cheap, to bidders from China and third-world countries. The equipment slowly floated from our shores to our global competitors. And now our engineering capability is joining it.

The last engineer standing goes unnoticed. By numbers, he's a shrinking and statically irrelevant percentage of the population. Yet we claim our engineering capability and its history of innovation is the muscle of our economic strength and hope for the future. What about the invention of the computer, the creation of Google, Apple, and Microsoft? A closer look at these companies does not bode well for the future. If we were privy to their five or ten-year plans, it would, of necessity, state the importance of something new, a product or new technology that does not exist today. For existing products, software development by expensive US engineers faces an increasing challenge: what new features will prompt a user to purchase a $120 upgrade to their operating system? The day is fast approaching, and some say it's here when IT departments at major corporations will say "No thanks" to Microsoft, "We don't need your new operating system release."

A software engineer once confided wistfully, "Not everyone can work at Google." The darling of Silicon Valley, ready to provide hot meals and childcare to its employees, is fueled by its advertising revenue. In that sense, it is parasitic on the economy's overall health. In an economic decline, the wind of payment goes out of their sails.

If the key to US future prosperity is innovation, and many agree that it is, then the belief that only the US has engineers like Steve Wozniak — the designer of the first Apple computer, is a fragile proposition. We once said that Japanese engineers could not innovate; they were too steeped in a culture of conformity. Tell that to the executives and stockholders of GM.

It's time to take our economic "ship" off autopilot, develop a strategic plan for the growth of US technology, and chart a course to a better destination before the "Made in America" product and its producers are relegated to history.

CHAPTER 50

PITTSBURGH

Pittsburgh in the fifties, and for several decades longer, was not a pretty city. It was a smokey, gritty, industrial city scared by strip mining and choked by billowing smokestacks of soot and pollution. The steam locomotives belched smoke and cinder ash, the sternwheeler river boats were coal-fired and dirty, and the steel mills lit the night sky in a backdrop of hazy smoke. Immigrant workers, mostly from eastern Europe, came here to find work, ... and they did. They became the laborers with "broad shoulders" who dug the coal from unsafe mines and did the hard work that made America strong and helped us beat the Germans. They carried lunch boxes, came home with dirty hands to their families, and lived a modest but proud life. Their home had three small bedrooms, one bath, and a large yard for a swing set and picnic table. They parked a new Chevy in a two-car garage and, every year, took a motor vacation to Erie or Niagara Falls, places away from the smoke and soot in their lives. They hoped for the future that their sons and daughters would graduate from high school, get married, and the young men would work in the mills as they did. Fourth of July fireworks, church festivals, studio wrestling on the black and white TV, and bottles of Iron City or Duquesne beer were the ingredients of a simple but good life.

But the mills are mostly gone, and for many older men, their hope is also gone. It started in the eighties when the steel mills became uncompetitive in the global marketplace. The unions blamed management, and management called the unions greedy. The men looked around and found little work and outdated skills in the new world economy. They were too old to learn computers, and no one had a good idea of what they could do. Factories closed as manufacturing moved overseas to Chinese factories where labor was cheaper. Their once beautiful buildings, churches, and banks started a long decay, and the men hunkered down to live quiet lives in the small towns up and down the Mon Valley, like Braddock, Mckeesport, Glassport, Clairton (the city of prayer), and Elizabeth.

As I drive the roads along the river and through these falling-down towns, I'm struck with how clean the air is, how blue the sky is, and how the tangled Pennsylvania vegetation is taking back the land. The strip mines, the old coal tipple, and the funnels of sunken land caused by collapsed coal mine timbers have been covered over, healed, and it takes on a tidy appearance unless you're near one of the abandoned factories, with all those tall, smokeless chimneys looking like cemetery markers for their death.

Pittsburgh is now an economy of "Ed." and "Med" and is slowly coming back to life with a new opportunity. Old infrastructure, a train station, has been turned into a tourist destination. And it's beautiful—everyone agrees. I'm happy about that part, although I remember a time when it was not pretty, there was a good life to be lived, and now that's gone. Time heals all, and as we hear in Walt Whitman's poem, The Leaves, "..I am the grass; I cover all."

CHAPTER 51

THE RICH NEED YOUR HELP

Storm clouds are gathering on our economic horizon. The number of rich who earn 25% of the income and control 40% of the wealth has diminished to a mere 1% of the population. This decreasing percentage could seriously impact our country's prosperity unless we do something to help the rich become more wealthy.

Why? We've been told that the rich create jobs, and for the remaining 99% of the population, jobs are what we need. US unemployment hovers in the 9% range, but for pockets of our people, it's much higher, for example, 25% among inner-city youth. There are signs that the rich are unhappy with their opportunity to become richer: they have moved their manufacturing off-shore. They have moved their corporate headquarters to small towns in Switzerland. If not helped, they might take the next step and push their households to Paris or Frankfurt, bringing their staff of cooks, maids, housekeepers, bodyguards, personal trainers, and event planners.

Republicans understand the issue. Some of them are in the 1% club and, not surprisingly, support the importance of helping the rich get richer. The liberal media and left-wing politicians don't understand that bashing a corporate executive's compensation makes them less likely to create US jobs. And it misses the point. For example, the safety performance bonus for the Horizon Deep Water rig managers is something to applaud. Imagine the consequences if **more** than one rig had exploded and poured millions of gallons of oil into the ocean.

The rich represent a small percentage of the population; their earnings are dwarfed by the remaining 75% of our income. It is in our interest to help them be more successful and happy—not to become guilt-ridden and ashamed. That's not easy. The rich can afford the best schools, live in the best neighborhoods, enjoy the best health care, and frankly, don't need the government to help them. A small government with fewer regulations, fewer taxes, and less meddling are preferred. Presently, those benefits are costly for them to attain: hiring lobbyists, making campaign contributions, and hosting dinners in their homes. That can be changed.

Aside from applauding their high salaries and country club memberships, we can look for more tangible ways to show appreciation. Although it's unlikely they would visit a national park, let's have a policy that the rich would move to the front of the line. Let's convert the under-used commuter lanes to "Affluent Lanes." Rich people would have a special license plate that signals their privileged status. Like immune diplomats, their speeding stops could be turned into an opportunity to get, for example, a Mark Zuckerberg autograph.

Rich people are better educated, better traveled, and in a position to create jobs and improve our well-being. It could be argued that they are also more intelligent. What else explains their privileged status? Let's give them more than one vote. A top-earning billionaire would have 1000 votes, a multi-millionaire 100 votes, and so on. Conversely, people living under the poverty line, unemployed, on welfare benefits, etc., should not be allowed to vote. It would incentivize them to "get off their duff," which the rich would appreciate.

Let's give the rich the comfort of living in a stable and peaceful society by helping the poor improve their lives in more realistic ways in today's economy. I'm sure the rich would agree to fund basketball and football training camps for inner-city youth. Let's expand the lottery program to allow more people to improve their quality of life. Let's reduce our investment in higher education because, frankly, the job opportunities for the highly educated are not bright. The money spent on education might be better directed to basic skills development in the service industry, something better aligned with today's job market.

It's not too late. In gratitude, the rich will support our priority to stop abortion, stop the spread of gay and lesbian marriage, put school prayer back in the classroom, send our soldiers over the globe to create democracy, and, best of all, support our image of a fiercely independent, patriotic American who needs no help—someone who can be as successful as his God-given belief in hard work takes him.

CHAPTER 52

URBAN GLEANER

A small, significantly older woman was opening and closing the lids of recycling bins in my condo complex. She struggled to reach inside one of the bins as I approached her. I took her three-foot stick with a nail protruding from its end—I don't remember if I took it or she handed it to me—and began fishing for returnables at the bottom of a recycling bin. It was too tall for her, her five-foot height barely reaching the top of the container, so I did the work, her nods, selecting or rejecting the items I recovered. I soon learned to look for soda and plastic bottles and ignore the wine and tin cans. Then we stuck gold: a plastic bag with a half dozen soda cans, each nested in but quickly removed from empty tins of soup and tomatoes.

She thanked me repeatedly, but I didn't know what to say. I felt guilty that several months earlier, I had taken her picture and posted it to Facebook with some clever caption I can't remember. It had made fun of her and these urban gleaners. Her actions had defied my understanding of the poor, but I now see that they have a currency of their own: metals and recyclables that can be sold for money to buy things they need. How many soda cans would it take to buy a loaf of bread in California ... or anywhere?

I had taken her picture with a telephoto lens from across the street, hiding behind my fence so she wouldn't see me, but now I was standing next to her and experiencing her toothless, smiling expression. She was dressed in clean clothes, not the stereotype of a down-and-out person. The scarf that covered her head, her brown, wrinkled skin, and her beatific expression reminded me of a nun. The socks on her sandaled feet didn't match. United by our common task, we tried to communicate. "I'm 88 years old," she said. I smiled and, wanting the conversation to continue, said, "I'm 71." Then she said she loved the Lord or the Lord loved her; I couldn't understand. I wanted to know her better, but her halting English would not allow a further connection between us.

We both smiled as the last bin was closed, and she slowly walked away—everything she did was slow. I wanted to imagine that she would return to a nearby home where she lived with a daughter or son. They would say, "Mom, you don't have to do that; we have enough." "I want to help," she might say. And they would have a meal and play with the children. Or her situation might be worse, something we don't want to imagine in this land of plenty.

As she moved out of view, I wondered if I had done enough to help her. A dollar from my wallet would have been more than her entire collection of cans. Sadly, I knew that nothing I could or was willing to do would significantly change her life. Then I thought about my situation. Are the six degrees of economic separation between us enough? Things can change. Maybe I'm not that far removed from her and the army of urban gleaners who pass silently through our lives.

Next time I'm going to ask where she lives.

CHAPTER 53

THERE ARE WHITE BUSSES IN HEAVEN

Dad, I want to be a Google engineer when I grow up. Son, not everyone can be a Google engineer; here, start reading this book, the "California Rules of the Road."

Dad, why are Google buses painted white? Son, It's because invisible paint hasn't been invented yet.

Here, put on this bike helmet ... and look both ways... unless it's a Google bus; they have deep pockets.

Mommy, why are there two white buses in a row? That's for former Tandem employees.

Mom, a lovely man, asked me to get on his white bus today. Is that okay? Of course, honey, those buses are free.

I'm tired of studying for the SAT. Son, do I need to take you on a white bus ride today? But dad, they have the same health plan.

How many white buses does it take to create a poor working backlash? Answer: one bus and one newspaper reporter.

Mom, I want to grow up and live in Oakland, the murder capital of the west, and take a shiny white bus to work every day. Brittany, dear, you know you'll get the weekends off.

What's the fastest-growing job opportunity in Silicon Valley? Healthcare. And next? Bus driver.

Where do all those white buses go at night, dad? Son, they park them in the cloud.

Dear, let's buy a bus, convert it to a motorhome, and tour the USA. Well, honey, it'll have to be some color other than white.

Old white buses never die; they get sold to startups.

If you placed every white bus end-to-end, you would cover the distance from San Francisco to Mountain View.

White buses are for thinkers, not lovers.

How many Google engineers does it take to release the next version of Android? Answer: about 60 white buses are full.

Adam and Eve entered the Garden of Eden, ate the forbidden fruit, and humanity spent the rest of their lives on a white bus.

How come there are no black Google buses? The roadway would look like a box of See's Candy.

Can Google engineers see out of their Google white bus windows? Yes, but they don't want to.

CHAPTER 54

COLLECTION: DEATH AND DYING

CHAPTER 55

THE ARC OF A MAN'S LIFE — THE LONELY JOURNEY FROM WOMB TO TOMB

Seldom discussed or written about, despite it happening to half of the population ... in some grand denial — like cancer, it's not a reality until the doctor pronounces it: the solitary journey that men take throughout their lives, from birth to death. The biological imperative to deliver sperm for the next generation has few requirements, especially in the modern world. Men, subconsciously aware of their diminished role, make futile attempts to attach significance to their post-game importance. On the other hand, women, having endured centuries of second-class citizenship, have developed a take-it-or-leave-it attitude about the importance and necessity of their husband's participation in creating and maintaining a "house & home" for their children. It's desired, it's appreciated, but it's no longer a necessity. And the last trump card, "I earn money, and what I say goes," is off the table.

The radio program "Father Knows Best" began in 1949 when the idea that a man knows what is best was thought to be true. And it morphed over the years into a TV series that passed from network to network until the show ended in 1960. In those waning years, the role of the father as family leader was changing, and no strong actor face with good teeth and a bow tie could maintain the changing reality in the American home. A man's opinion today is a "data point," and it may be believed or ignored. The larger world has invaded the family to its core, and social media now influence the decisions made by wives and family, peer opinion tweeted at the speed of light, and evolving societal norms—norms that take the male off the throne and into the crucible with the rest of the family.

For a male child, the long journey after leaving his mother's breast and, soon after, her hand is a solo adventure with little navigational help. A boy is handed an action toy, a weapon (or a violent video game), some sports equipment, and a ride by mom to a venue of boys tussling each other for dominance. Tough it up and never cry is dad's advice, and mom defers to him, lest the boy grows up weak and unable to compete. It will take years of self-learning for the boy-to-man to return to the breast and intimacy with women and his wife and to win success in the competitive economic landscape. It won't be easy, not like his grandfather, whose life was laid out like a suit of clothes: high school diploma / marry high school sweetheart / get mill job / buy a house and car / have 2-3 kids / take an auto trip once a year to Lake Erie.

Boys compete at every level, and there is little benefit to sharing the "game" details with a male friend. A claim of getting "laid" is a lie away. Moments of intimate sharing or unvarnished honesty might be considered crossing the rigid line of being a male. This kind of "wiring" is formed for short-term success, not the long years after establishing a family, working on getting ahead, and eventually, retirement.

With some luck, men pass through these early wickets of life successfully but soon discover their emotional connection with their wives has waned; she increasingly has shifted her attention from courtship and affection to child-rearing. And with so many women working and pursuing their careers, the hearth is likely to be cold when he arrives home. It's the beginning of a drift to further solitude, and many men never make another emotional connection in their remaining life.

War changes everything, and it doesn't matter if it's a "good" war, like WW II, or a "dirty" war like Vietnam. It doesn't matter if it's a volunteer Army or the draft. It only matters that men are taken out of their role as husbands, fathers, and breadwinners and put at high personal risk with other men. Connection is survival. Relationships cut deep, and the barriers of male-to-male competition give way to bonds that promote mutual survival. These high stakes take men to feel love and affection for each other in a context with no shame or sexual ambiguity.

And for those who survived and came home, the longing for the intimacy of male companionship led to the creation of groups like the VFW (veterans of foreign wars) and various Vietnam Veterans groups. After WW II, men's organizations were formed or joined to provide venues for men to associate, like the Loyal Order of the Moose, The Elks, The Shriners, and in rural areas, Volunteer Fireman's Groups, The Grange, and rifle clubs.

Over time most of these organizations have died, like the men who fought in WW II. Urbanization and moving from real to virtual connections have left men with few opportunities to form deep relationships. There are exceptions in some professions, like police officers, firefighters, and paramedics. Still, for the most part, men have become loners who gather sports information to proffer with other lonely men in shallow discussions.

Sports fulfill the male thirst for battle and can be experienced in a safe, surrogate way, so much so that the broadcasting of sporting events is big business and fills the TV screen night and day. But the TV commercial of a tailgate party in a stadium parking lot is fiction for most men. Parking fees, football ticket prices, and massive traffic jams can be avoided by watching the game on their 65-inch TV. Sitting alone, with a bucket of chicken wings, a beer, and wearing a sports jersey, men try to relive the fierceness of the battle, the struggle, the teamwork, and the closeness to other men, who like them, need a solid emotional and physical connection to survive and win. This temporary connection is abruptly over when the screen goes dark.

Aging men, with less testosterone, their competitive working life over, and now having the time to pursue a different path, are ill-equipped for this new phase of life. They are unprepared for a new door opening, and society has marginalized them, stripped them of venues to associate with, and put them on a lonely path for the rest of their lives. For many, the long arc of their life ends on a solitary way to death.

CHAPTER 56

RUNNING OUT OF TIME: MY CHINESE CLOCK SAYS SO

I'm standing in front of my Walmart clock, shiny and freshly landed from its boat ride from China, and imagining it's a countdown clock for my journey to the other side. People say "the other side," but I don't believe that. No, it's a countdown to nothingness. If there were another side, it would be comforting to imagine a better place, and it would be distracted me from the incessant second-by-second progression of time. But here I am, watching the second hand traverse the short spaces between second "tics" on the clock face.

My engineer's mind sees into the guts of the clock: a quartz oscillator, a simple counter related to the magic "60" of universal time, and a stepper motor, advancing the gears one part of a revolution at a time. I hold on to my engineering thoughts as if they could anchor me to the world of the living. And it helps, for a while, until the sweeping second-hand pulls me back to the tic-tic. It's relentless.

Cosmology describes a universe that is accelerating at an ever-increasing rate. To where? More space? As a boy, staring at the night sky, I tried to imagine the edge of freedom: the boundary between space and no space. And in all my life, and now approaching 80, I still can't imagine the edge of an infinite universe, and I'm angry about that. If all living things have an end, if I have a lot, then why is the universe exempted from this rule?

A few moments pass, tic - tic, and It occurs to me that the real question is the one that mirrors my life. Like me, the universe has a clock, and it's ticking. In the end, mass reverts to energy and forms clouds, awaiting their rebirth in one infinitesimal "big bang." I was there, or at least a part of me, for the last birth, and I will be there for the next. The lines of Joni Mitchell's Woodstock song come to mind, "we are stardust." Finally, I know what the "other side" means—it's rebirth.

My eyes focus on the moving second hand. It has mysteriously jumped ahead, almost making a complete revolution. I want a time out to stop the clock, like in football. It would be free time, not counting that I could learn more about my journey. Enjoy a laugh or two or a good meal. But there is no stopping that oscillator, no pause button. I'm on a countdown.

I stare intently, watching the second hand make small movements for as long as possible. The Chinese clock keeps ticking; it doesn't know it has a battery and will die soon, just like me.

CHAPTER 57

CROSSING THE LINE

If you live long enough, you will eventually witness a close friend or acquaintance take that first tentative step over the line between living and dying. It's not a dramatic moment; maybe you have missed the signs for a long time, but now you know their mind and body have started that last journey, and there is no calling back.

The trajectory of every life has an endpoint. At first and for a long time, it's too distant to see or think about. As time and energy go by, gradually, it becomes visible. When you hear their goodbye (or resignation), your instinct is to rally them to life, to encourage them to hold on, but your words echo with no reinforcement.

If you wonder if life prepares you for death, rest assured that it does. When someone has been battered by sickness or hardship, when their burden becomes too heavy to carry and their days too empty and meaningless, when the excitement of the banal is too mute to find meaning, it's not hard for them to raise their hand and begin saying goodbye.

At first, you are sad for your friend and more so for yourself; you want to hold on to them and slow or stop their journey. Eventually, you begin to appreciate that it's better to let them go and imagine their burden being lifted. Walk with them as far as you can. That final goodbye will be easier for both of you.

CHAPTER 58

FALLING

Kahil Gibran writes that children are like arrows, shot from birth into the world, implying that a parent's influence is just the aiming and that the child/arrow will take its path. And so, as we shoot out, our lives are not a straight line; they have an ascendancy and a descent, and just as every song or story follows an arc to an inevitable denouement, so do we. Being subject to gravity, we may leave the earth, but only momentarily; gravity will pull us back. Somewhere along that path, we will, barring the possibility of stepping in front of a bus or having a cancer cell decide to multiply, find ourselves at the tipping point. There's no more up; it's an inevitable path down. This tipping point is sometimes hard to call; it's an extended, seemingly flat portion of the arc where we are going along, with no change in altitude. It may be the years after the children are raised or the challenges of work have been mastered, but inevitably, there will be a day when the call has to be made: we are falling. The journey is not over; there is still flight, but the falling back is felt, the ground is getting closer, and the destination is more and more in sight. How will we know? Sometimes our bodies will tell us; that it has been a long journey, and we have been buffeted by life, tossed around, and it will show. Sometimes it will be a subtle shift in orientation, a glance downward, a focus on where we have been, and a feeling that control is being lost. While others are still shooting upward, we are being left behind. We fall off their trajectory and look around at friends who have also done so, taking some comfort that we are falling together. It's time to tidy up and prepare for the landing. It may be throwing out old clothes, finally completing that family album, sorting through your tools, or making a last attempt to enjoy the view, to enjoy the remaining altitude, to shut your eyes and imagine floating.

CHAPTER 59

GROWING OLD WITH MIRRORS

Red wine and whiskey are said to improve with age, but not much else does. Buy a new car and drive it off the lot. It's not improving; it's immediately starting the long process of wearing out. Check with Kelley to observe how painful that can be. A pair of good leather shoes, Ferragamo's, for example, will improve with wearing until the time comes when a "Cat's Paw" heel and sole will not save the day.

And so we watch everything new, just out of the box, inextricably losing its luster and beginning to decay, or worse, falling apart, right before our eyes. Possessions that are "holding up" are declining at a rate we can't observe daily. But they are. We shed worn-out objects constantly, leaving a trail like dragon scales. In years past, an entity could wear out. Today, it only "wears out" its usefulness. Then, whatever remaining life it has may be given a second chance at the Good Will, but most likely, it will join its friends at the landfill to wait for an archeological dig. What sense will be made from the decayed remains of a popcorn air popper? A water-pic? A heated shaving cream dispenser? A yogurt maker?

This situation is so common that we attach special significance to anything that appears to stay constant (not getting better and not declining). If we are brutally honest, that list would also be concise. Even a gold ring will wear away slowly. A statue, painting, or fresco can suffer from the ravages of time, humidity, and toxic air if we are not careful. Perhaps a girl's best thing, a diamond, is an example of an immutable object. Along with cockroaches, they will survive until the next big bang.

On the other hand, people have a brief period of ascendency before a decline, sure as gravity, begins. A shaving mirror can't be trusted to inform; the family reunion, the birthday photograph, tells the story. We unconsciously observe each other and, spoken or not, note the ravages of time, the slackening of the jaw that telegraphs how everyone around us is aging. "You look good," may be said, but what isn't said is, "for a man in his seventies that had a heart attack." It's an innocent act of kindness, and we expect it will be reciprocated in good measure. And why not? We all travel the same journey of hair loss, wrinkled skin, and diminished energy. We call it the "glow" of living life, the wrinkle lines of character and experience, and the stoop from carrying a heavy burden nobly.

Despite the evidence, we may still see ourselves as a boy who could walk the railroad track, balanced on the rail, or a girl who could wear a size four dress and heels. It's partly denial and partly the desire to imagine that our experience is different, for to accept our decline is to get our death. We fight it at the gym, with wrinkle cream, or maybe the knife, if we can afford it. Our society is youth-centered to such an extreme that a forty-year-old person is pushed off the bus. The media populates our societal images with the faces of teenagers or the mask of makeup and Botox on someone older. No wonder it's difficult to accept our aging when no one else will. We may tell ourselves that we are wiser, have better judgment, or are better lovers, but that's a consolation, not a cause for celebration.

In their extraordinary benevolence, women grant men a pass for aging and can appreciate a man's kindness and character despite sagging skin and a big paunch. You would believe such service would be reciprocated, but, alas, men tyrannize women with the expectation that they must always look girl-young and present themselves with the exaggerated features of sexual signaling. Red lips, perky, large breasts on a thin body, high heels, and flawless skin are the measure of worthiness and attractiveness. A Ph.D. from Harvard is not part of the formula.

The tyranny continues for too long until one day, the man wakes up with a low "T" and decides to give up the illusion that he's still in the game. Similarly, at some point in her life, a woman decides to stop playing a losing game and live. It may sound like resignation, but it's a liberation—the permission to be happy at the moment.

Aging "sucks." We will all get through it with compassion for our fellow man and a heart open to matters of genuine substance. But it still sucks.

CHAPTER 60

LAST CURTAIN CALL

The stage lights are still blazing, but soon the last curtain call will extinguish them, the theater will go dark, and your name will be removed from the marquee. The performance is over; your life is over. A few reprises and some good luck will extend the run, but the show permanently closes. If we are lucky, it's swift and merciful. If not, the final act is a tragedy for you and everyone involved.

We don't get to choose, do we? Or maybe we do? We make infinite choices along the way—to smoke or not smoke, hit the booze, skip the exercise. Deepak Chopra proffers these choices as life-affirming opportunities, and they are, but the payoff may be too far in the future for many folks to make that gamble and live a more conservative life.

I live in a retirement community, a luxury halfway house on the other side. The lucky ones buzz around in golf carts and take bus tours to museums. The less fortunate ones push walkers from a door drop-off to the dining room and then back home to watch TV. It's fenced and guarded by gunless, uniformed guards that keep the timid from entering this theme park for the aged.

The absence of anyone under 45 years in the community suggests a science fiction movie where the last vestige of human civilization is destined to die off, the last survivors too old to procreate.

But we solder on, hanging out in the pools and hot tubs, telling our life stories to strangers. They remember Howdy Doody and Milton Burl, Jack Par and Lucile Ball, and like me, grew up before television and computers. We all agree that failing to teach cursive writing in schools is a tragedy, and tattoos are ugly and a desecration of the body.

Soon, parboiled by the hot tub, we leave, and new people arrive to talk about the last good war, the time they visited Paris and could walk the Champs Elysees at night without fear. There is rarely talk about the future beyond the next ukulele club meeting.

If we were honest, we'd admit that we are no longer in the parade, no longer on the sidelines watching the parade, and don't care anymore about the parade. We're holding our bodies together to eek as much pleasure as possible before the wheelchair, and the medical supply company delivers all the other medical devices.

We may be the lucky ones. We destroyed the planet with our greed and helped create a have-and-have-not society through our complicity with the moneyed interests. We have failed democracy and a president that is a lying moron, but as luck would have it, we get to hide out in our gated community. It's too high in the hills to worry about coastal flooding and too protected and insular to be exposed to poor people and street crime.

The worst thing that could happen is that the pump on the hot tub will fail ... again.

CHAPTER 61

LETTERS FROM HOSPICE

"Mr. Watson, it's been hard reaching you. Is this your new home?"

"I see... hospice, and how is that for you?"

"That's nice. I'm glad you're okay because I've been trying to reach you to let you know we can extend the warranty on your 2007 Prius."

"But first, we need to update our records. Is this a temporary or permanent address change?"

"Okay, temporary. Please let us know when you have a new permanent address."

"Is this a good phone number to reach you during the day?"

"About your car, sir, you know a large repair could set you back financially and maybe cause you to miss some work, especially if you don't have a rental car benefit. Have you considered that your older car will need expensive repairs, and have you considered what your time is worth?"

"You don't drive anymore?" Your niece?

"Sir, we can extend the warranty for her. I'm sure you would have peace of mind knowing that she will not be financially burdened because you didn't want to spend a few dollars on her behalf. We have a payment plan with no-interest payments over six months. Can I sign you up?"

"You need time to think about it. Yes, I can stay on the line. My lunch break is starting in a few minutes."

"I'm 23 years old ... and ... I'm not married. I want to meet someone, but to be honest, I have a tough time with relationships. Can I ask a question? Why are you in hospice?"

"I've never heard of that. I'm sure you will beat it. I read somewhere that your mind can cure disease, especially if we have a positive attitude."

"No, I don't date. My mom said I was doomed to be a loner. You know, she died of cancer when I was pretty young."

"Maybe they'll find a cure for what you have. We need one of those telethons to get some money."

"Mom was only 43. She was divorced, and her dad was never around. It was tough for her. I tried to do my best, but Jesus, I couldn't be her husband. I mean, I was just a kid."

"No sir, I'm not allowed to bring the paperwork to your hospice. I have to mail it."

"Yes, I've enjoyed talking to you."

"I could get into much trouble. Your address, is it your address?"

"Hang in there, Mr. Watson. My mom said it's always the darkest before the dawn."

Goodbye, sir.

CHAPTER 62

LOGAN'S RUN FOR SENIORS

A few minutes after nine AM, the Mall doors have just opened, and the "Mall-Walkers" are already circling the labyrinthine mall interior. Rain or shine, winter or summer, they gather in groups of two or three, their coats and purses stashed in lockers and outfitted in loose-fitting clothing and "safe" shoes — sneakers from Wal-Mart or the "nun" shoes advertised in the back of AARP magazine — they begin the daily ritual. Not to be mistaken for an actual shopper, these senior "Chariots of Fire" never glance at the window displays or the signs promising "going out of business" bargains. Except for food and medicine, their days of consumption are over.

With the pleasure of coffee and conversation waiting after the walk, the mall has become the senior center for those still walking. Sure footing and pleasant temperatures compensate for the enjoyment of a tree or bird in flight. And besides, time at the mall saves the expense of heating or cooling their home.

Watching them "orbiting" the mall, I'm reminded of the 1976 Movie, "Logan's Run." A box-office flop, it has become a cult film for sci-fi fans expecting a dark future of economic malaise and "big-brother" control of our lives. In a post-apoplectic world, anyone over 30 years old is sent to "Carousal" to be terminated, with the false promise of resurrection.

They're smiling. In the senior citizen version, I'm observing that the age has been raised, but it's the same outcome.

One day "Mary" will disappear from the group.

"Where's Mary? I haven't seen her in a few weeks."

"Someone said she had a stroke; she's in a convalescent home somewhere."

"We should go to visit her sometime."

"Yeah, that would be nice."

The ranks will close, and life will go on for those waiting for the next turning event in the tricky business of dying.

CHAPTER 63

MUSICAL CHAIRS

A cruel game we play our whole life.

Remember the first time you played musical chairs? You were a kid, maybe in kindergarten or the first grade, and your teacher lined up the chairs and got out the record player. When the needle dropped, the class circled the chairs. You paused in front of each chair, hoping you would have a place to sit when the music stopped. Sometimes you and a classmate descended upon the same chair and your chances of claiming it flew out the window unless you were more extensive or aggressive and could push the other child away.

There weren't enough chairs for everyone; one child would unceremoniously leave the game each time it was played, and then a chair would be removed. It was designed to have you fail at some point. The inevitability quickly penetrated your young brain. Some kids sensed it immediately and gave up; others played more aggressively and were determined to claim the last chair. They were the kids who would run companies and hold public office. You and most other kids found yourselves somewhere in the middle of this dilemma, knowing that the game was rigged but accepting that it was the *only* game. You played but rarely won.

It wasn't your fault. The perpetrator of the game, your teacher, and your parents didn't prepare you to win. They taught you to be polite, share, and feel you deserve their love unconditionally. It was never a contest to select winners and losers. But life had something else in mind. At home, you competed with a brother or sister for your mother's attention or with her chores and distractions to "win" some time to receive her affection. That game at school, out in the real world, only confirmed that you would spend your whole life playing and often losing.

The idea that there is not enough to go around is pervasive in everything we do. In those grade school years, our classmates were our friends, but we learned they were also our enemies in getting a chair or something else we wanted. Life pits us against each other. It's not personal (even though we often feel that way), and as we move through our lives, we settle in a chair of some description. It may not be the best chair, probably not, and certainty not the one we wanted. We nevertheless hold on to it because it's all we have. It would be not kind to take it away, … but life does.

In the recent recession, our economic "chairs" were cleared away. As a nation, we circled what few chairs were remaining, competing with our neighbors and friends for jobs and a place to sit at the table. As a society, we were pitted in a game where age, good looks, education, privilege, and, yes, some luck determined the winners. Nevertheless, we expected that slowly the chairs would be brought back—the game had always worked that way. We were wrong. Not only were they removed, but what was brought back was not the same chair, job, or even close.

Millions of people have given up and have stopped playing. The remaining have kids, mortgages, braces, and dreams and are too young to give up, but they are finding new "furniture" on the playing field. The full-time job has been replaced by seasonal help, part-time employment, temp jobs, low-paying service industry jobs, and so on. Wages are depressed, benefits trimmed or non-existent. Somewhere deep in the recession, companies figured out how to run their business with less help, a different kind of help, or help from cheaper workers in other countries. For the first time in memory, the prospects of a diminished lifestyle are being fulfilled. Worse, the opportunities for our children are not much better. They have more time to prepare for the new world order, but the "not enough to go around" factor has heightened the competition and pitted them fiercely against each other.

Ironically, and staying with the metaphor, there is enough wood, fabric, and stuffing for everyone to have a chair. However, with greed ruling the day, the game has turned bitter, pitting a small class of the wealthy against a growing class of the disenfranchised. Words like "taker" and "lazy" describe people playing a rigged game. Politicians kindle the flames in the hope of gaining an advantage.

Unlike the "harmless" school game of musical chairs, today's game has descended to survival. Empathy, never a good strategy for winning has left the field.

CHAPTER 64

ON DEATH AND DYING

On Death and Dying Birth and death, the bookends of our lives, are a mere heartbeat in the life of the cosmos, yet we struggle to live our lives fully in what seems like a long journey of twists and turns. Joni Mitchell, the poet laureate of my generation, expressed it succinctly in the lyrics of her song, "Hejira:"

....
We all come and go unknown.
Each so deep and superficial
Between the forceps and the stone
....

I'm at the age that if I died, a surviving friend might say, "He led a full life," No one would say, "He was too young to die." I couldn't stand at the pearly gates in the afterlife and claim my life was cut short. Having gone this far, I've reached a time when death is not very far removed from my world, and the prospects of getting in the closet for a dark suit for a friend or relative's funeral are increasing all the time. I also know that someone in my family may need to reach into my closet for me, but I try not to dwell on it.

We start life in a birth dance with our mother; we need each other to make it happen, and doctors are called in when one or the other is not making an effort. In stark contrast, we are alone when we take the last step and cross the line between life and death, either as an act of our will, a statement by the body that it can go no further, or both. No one knows; there are no experts on dying (and what difference would it make?). The room may be full of friends and relatives, but they are not going with you. They are the people on the dock, waving and crying as you sail away. Their tears are not all about you; some will call because you have, for a moment, reminded them that they too will make the same journey, and the inevitably of their death frightens them.

After you're gone, your death's short tear in the fabric of the universe will soon repair after the baggies of jewelry are divided among the granddaughters after the clothes are sorted, and most are taken to the Good Will. After a place is found for your old slide rule or collection of Dutch figurines, the healing will begin. Soon, any mention of you will be reserved for family gatherings or the funerals of those who have outlasted you. "Bill would have liked this" may be the highest compliment in your life.

It would be arrogant to think it should be any other way. We all die; at best, whatever mark we make is merely a scratch. It can be no other way because, in the broader perspective of life, we only matter to the few people who surround us, and those people will also die. It has taken me too long to learn that life is, for better or worse, what you create with friends and family in your immediate world and a little more. Your joy, laughter, and tears are alive there, and that alone is the meaning of life. For those who wait for the next life and in the waiting do not fully invest in this one, I say your life is a tragedy of one not fully lived.

You may wonder what a person my age feels about dying. The idea of not dying isn't an option. I can tell you that perhaps not now, but over time, acceptance of death can bring peace. What young people don't know is that dying is a lifelong, slow-motion process. Moving through life, we acquire a thousand cuts that will eventually have their way. Any single amount is not the end ... or so it seems. Losing the ability to do a handstand is no big deal. The inability to play a tennis game is not a big deal. Eventually, the wheelchair or walker seems like a good idea because we can still get around. We believe death is like the jam in Alice in Wonderland: jam yesterday and jam tomorrow, but never jam today.

Will the day ever come when you are ready to die? Take this test. Tell your family not to worry and then drive your car to a hilltop with a good view. Turn off the motor and see how long you can stay there. At first, you may enjoy the view and look around to enjoy its beauty. After a short while, your ability to absorb beauty to any greater depth is gone, and you start to think about a chore that needs to be done or being there when your kids come home from soccer practice. The pull of your life below will become an irresistible force that will move you to turn the key and drive away.

Now, imagine someone older, someone, with an illness or medical condition, driving to that exact spot. He has seen better views, in fact, many spectacular views—maybe the grand canyon—and this one has no interest. That alone will not cause him to turn the key. It's the fact that nothing below pulls to him. He has made love, gotten drunk, worked a good job, and done all the stuff that makes up a life, and now that's over, there is nowhere else to go, nothing more to do. He may turn the car toward home because his body is still in this world, but he has said goodbye and is ready to leave. When that day comes, you will know too if it is your fate.

CHAPTER 65

THE WAY THE WORLD ENDS

Karl Marx once said, "religion is the opiate of the people." We get the idea. The church's strategy to keep the masses uneducated created an obedient population of believers who were entertained and willing to support the church coffers completely. Later, a new religion emerged. Borrowing Marx's phrase, Edward R Murrow commented that "television is the opiate of the people." The networks feed us a "drug" as influential as any needle in the arm. Fast forward to today and look around, and opiates are everywhere. TV is fading to irrelevance; one more reality show may be its death. It's of no concern; we have moved on to our X-Box, iPad, Twitter account, Roku box, and endless messaging about everything we do, even bodily functions. "Wait a sec; I have to put the phone down and wipe." None of these opiates are in themselves wrong or bad. No, it's the lingering ignorance that goes with such distractions. It's our willingness to numb out, dumb down, and enjoy the flesh of the last animal facing extinction.

With a nod to TS Elliot's poem, "The Hollow Men," This is the way the earth ends; This is the way the earth ends; This is the way the world ends; Not with a bang but a Twitter.

CHAPTER 66

COLLECTION: WAR

CHAPTER 67

D DAY

It was seventy years ago, I'm in another life, and I'm standing, no, lurching in an LSA on the way to Omaha Beach. It's early morning; a mist hangs over the water and the distant cliffs. No one is talking, we're done with that, and it's too noisy, and what is there to say? We're all going to die, or most of us. It's the only conclusion in this unprobable assault on the fortified German Normandy coastline. Somehow there is peace in that; the effort to survive can be given up, and we command our bodies to move forward, as we did in the ongoing training that went into this day. Now it's the real thing, and whatever shred of a life I have, other than war, is gone, maybe forever.

I don't know Hitler or a single German person. Nor do I know any French person in the towns near Normandy who would be grateful for this sacrifice, who would cook a meal and kiss me on the cheek. There is so much I don't know other than the draft notice, long train rides, and waiting. I'm a simple person, I've never hated anyone enough to kill, and now I have a gun and orders to kill every German I can. I'm sure the Germans soldiers have the exact charges. How are we different? Who wins this soldier game?

There was never a point in my ideological grooming to be a killer that I could have raised my hand to say, "No, I don't think I can do that." My home and my factory job in Pittsburgh were never threatened. No, this war is a world away in Europe, where I have been taken to make things right. My mind cannot make the connection.

In truth, somewhere in the training camp, in a classroom where I was taught to field-strip and reassemble my MI rifle, I gave up any need for understanding. We all did. A soldier doesn't need to understand. How would that help? The only decision I have left is when to pull the trigger.

Some men are vomiting. Their undigested breakfast splatters on the floor, mixing with the seawater splashing over the gunnels. This is not a real boat. No boat would ever be built this way. It is a death boat. It has only one purpose: deliver me to the shore, if possible, so that I can kill Germans.

I know the other 29 men, some more, some less. We have become a family in a short time, and we love each other and will cry when we see a buddy's dead body. The only thing that matters now is helping each other survive. We will do that, but as I jump off the open landing door, I sink in water up to my chest and am entirely alone. It's cold, and my gear is heavy. I don't want to die. I want to give up, but I continue. I'm almost to the shore. My last thoughts are of the small town in Pittsburgh and the people who will miss me.

CHAPTER 68

TENTH ANNIVERSARY OF THE IRAQ WAR

Looking back at my time in the army, I never had a bullet whizz past my head, heard an explosion nearby, never had to help a bleeding friend on the ground. I didn't need to go into the Army—no peer ever did. And for that brief time, no politician, no general saw the need to send me to die somewhere far from home. For that, I can write this and salute all those who were not so lucky.

In 1964 I ran from the Army, burned or gave away my uniforms, saving only a fatigue jacket with a white patch that read, "WATSON." My kids would later wear it on Halloween. A helmet and toy guy would transform them into something we could laugh about: a kid in a military uniform with a gun. When the Army delivered my household goods from Germany, it produced souvenirs from a happy time driving around Germany in my sports car. The wine glasses, lead crystal, tapestries, and hand-knit sweaters were a modest price, including a few Deutsch Marks. I had no scars, missing limbs, or post-traumatic stress disorder and suffered no sleepless nights.

I went back to school and forgot about being a soldier. My questions about why we had so many troops worldwide were quickly forgotten. When the Vietnam war raged on and on, I ignored it. The news reports were repetitive, and battle scenes were from a movie set. I never questioned why we were there; just thankful I was out of the Army, and it had been just in time. I never imagined the flotilla of boats it would take to remove over fifty thousand bodies from a distant country none of us would ever visit. I didn't imagine the hundreds of thousands of wives, parents, and relatives who would grieve the rest of their lives, the empty chairs, the bedroom shrine that would never be slept in again, and all the lives that would never be lived.

And now I am old, the last one to give a hand in the next war. For the last ten years, I have sat in my comfortable living room, watching the images of dead young men and women in silence. It's the public television's honor role of those who have given their lives, but for what, I am thinking. They are the faces of kids from small towns I have never heard of, towns where the factories are closed, and there is not much opportunity, towns where the flags from 9/11 are still flying, and the "USA" decals are still on their old cars.

In all this time, I have never seen a politician or general's face on my large screen. They remain in Washington or the safety of a compound far from danger. Suppose I ever hear again the words that the world is a better place because we invaded Iraq. In that case, I want to take that person, in a modern version of a Dickens's story, to a Thanksgiving table in one of those small towns, to sit in the chair where a son or daughter once sat, to help them say a prayer of Thanksgiving.

If God created heaven and earth and us in His image in seven days, why couldn't He have taken just one more day, one more day, to give us enough wisdom to know that it is always wrong to kill each other?

CHAPTER 69

MEMORIAL DAY 2022

Memorial Day is a day off from work. A chance to have a barbecue, go to the beach, or be with the family and have a quiet day.

We may hear a sound bite from a Biden speech honoring all the soldiers who have died to keep our country free and to preserve our democracy. The news may show a parade with flags waving and a marching band playing a military song. We may feel a sense of pride in being an American and are grateful for all their sacrifice.

For all the wives, mothers, brothers, sisters, and relatives of men who died in Korea, Vietnam, Afghanistan, Iraq, and military training accidents, we tell the same lie year after year: your loved one failed to keep us free. It would be too cruel. He died, for now, reason at all. In no tangible way can we assign the preservation of our liberty to your loved one dying.

Almost 37,000 soldiers died in the frozen lands of Korea, wearing inadequate clothing left over from WW II. Please remind me why.

And the 58,000 soldiers who died in Vietnam. Drafted to fight in a country no one had been to or would ever go to. In rice patties and aircraft shot from the air. Breathing agent orange and bringing drug addiction home. They were then shunned by society for fighting a stupid, unpopular war. Many soldiers died so that we could save face. How did that make us free?

The 2,400 died in Afghanistan. Were you doing what? And what for?

And the 4,600 soldiers died in Iraq because we thought they had nuclear weapons. How are we safer and sleep more accessible because of that war?

Politicians declare war; soldiers die in battle. If we keep telling the lie year after year, the windows and relatives of dead soldiers will have no voice, and the subsequent war to save democracy will be easy to justify.

There was never an immediate threat of invasion of America, yet we sent 405,000 of our young men to their death in foreign lands. I don't justify war, but I think we did the right thing. So on Memorial Day, I truly believe they fought for freedom and democracy. But for every war since then, we killed our young men for no good or justifiable reason. None. And don't try to tell me they died to keep us free.

In my mind, Memorial Day is to take a day to acknowledge that the United States is dying. We are no longer the greatest nation in the world (Aaron Sorken's words spoken by Jeff Bridges in Newsroom). Our long history of killing Indians, Filipinos, and Mexicans and purchasing men from Africa to do our work had corrupted our morality to the breaking point. The world's wealthiest nation has populations of people who can't feed themselves or get medical attention. Do we tell another lie that it's a poor person's fault they can't succeed?

And we are so polarised and divisive that we can elect a draft-dodging man who tells a lie after lie? And wants to make us great again. Another lie that millions and millions of people firmly believe.

I'm not looking forward to veteran's day.

CHAPTER 70

STICK ENVY

America has lost its "stick." Somewhere along the path of two wars, four thousand dead men and women, and twelve years of pouring treasure into foreign lands, we've lost our "stick." John McCain, Linsey Graham, and Newt Gingrich—if ever there was a reason to have gay marriage approved nationwide—(and many other republicans) are experiencing "sick envy" of Russia's Putin and, amazingly, accuse our black president of having no "stick."

They suggest we take some "military viagra" and provide arms and military support to Ukraine. Imagine a large ship arriving (where?) and tons of tanks, guns, and ammo being unloaded in Ukraine. How about some military advisors teach them how to maintain and shoot those weapons? Let's widen their airport runways, build a few more roads and bridges, and build a few schools and hospitals to gain community support. Never mind that our infrastructure is falling apart, our schools are too costly for the 99% to attend, and we can't afford to help our returning veterans.

Maybe Ukraine is the place to draw a line in the dirt and prove that our "stick" is bigger than Putin's. Bush- Chaney had (or still has) a big "stick" that worked well. Or maybe we got it backward; perhaps they had a small "stick" and tried to fake it? Many dead warriors aren't around to enter the debate about whether our military "stick" made the world better by toppling Saddam Hussein's statue.

I can see the 2016 election will have a new litmus test: "how big is your "stick?" How will that work for Hillary? We would have a better America if a woman became president, and we could take testosterone out of geopolitical politics. Maybe Graham- McCain will retire and take their "stick" suggestions to the senior center. I hear the men over there need help.

CHAPTER 71

TOO OLD FOR THE NEXT WAR

Looking back at my time in the army, I never had a bullet whizz past my head, heard an explosion nearby, never had to help a bleeding friend. I didn't need to go into the Army—no peer ever did. When I did, as a wet-behind-the-ears 2nd Lieutenant, no politician, no general saw the need to send me to die somewhere far from home. For that, I can write this and salute all those who were not so lucky.

In 1964 I ran from the Army, burned or gave away my uniforms, saving only a fatigue jacket with a white patch that read, "WATSON." My kids would later wear it on Halloween. A helmet and toy guy would transform them into something we could laugh about: a kid in a military uniform with a gun. When the Army delivered my household goods from Germany, it produced souvenirs from a happy time driving around Germany in my sports car. The wine glasses, lead crystal, tapestries, and hand-knit sweaters were gotten at a modest price, a few Deutsch Marks, and were greeted as war loot by my parents when the large shipping crate arrived. I had no scars, missing limbs, or post-traumatic stress disorder and suffered no sleepless nights.

I went back to school and forgot about being a soldier. My questions about why we had so many troops worldwide were quickly forgotten. When the Vietnam war raged on and on, I ignored it. The news reports were repetitive, and battle scenes were from a movie set. I never questioned why we were there; just thankful I was out of the Army, and it had been just in time. I never imagined the flotilla of boats it would take to remove over fifty thousand bodies from a distant country none of us would ever visit. I didn't imagine the hundreds of thousands of wives, parents, and relatives who would grieve the rest of their lives, the empty chairs, the bedroom shrine that would never be slept in again, and all the lives that would never be lived.

And now I am old, the last one to give a hand in the next war. For the last ten years, I have sat in my comfortable living room watching the PBS images of dead young men and women in silence. It's the public television's honor role of those who have given their lives, but for what, I am thinking. They are the faces of kids from small towns I have never heard of, towns where the factories are closed, and there is not much opportunity, towns where the flags from 9/11 are still flying, and the "USA" decals are still on their old cars.

In all this time, I have never seen a politician or general's face on my large screen. They remain in Washington or the safety of a compound far from danger. Suppose I ever hear again the words that the world is a better place because we invaded Iraq. In that case, I want to take that person, in a modern version of a Dickens's story, to a Thanksgiving table in one of those small towns, to sit in the chair where a son or daughter once sat, to help them say a prayer of Thanksgiving.

If God created heaven and earth and us in His image in seven days, why couldn't He have taken just one more day, one more day, to give us enough wisdom to know that it is consistently wrong to kill each other?

CHAPTER 72

VETERANS DAY 2018

I'm a veteran, having served two years as a second lieutenant in the Army Signal Corps in Germany, But I'm not a hero; I don't even come close. I consider myself a Vietnam *survivor* by NOT serving during the Vietnam War—I was in and out by 1964, well before the loss of 58,000 American soldiers began. I'm convinced I would be part of that total had it not been for the timing of my birth. I had no reservations about serving my country.

But the America that existed in 1962 doesn't exist to anyone, and I'm not proud of who we are now (you reading this are the exception). No friend of mine ever served. Deferments keep them from harm's way, like our current president and commander-in-chief. And during my service, I never carried or shot a weapon.

In 1962 it was just two decades after millions of Jews were slaughtered during WW II, yet I sat with Germans in restaurants as is the custom in that country. And now, I would not sit with millions of Americans who hate immigration, gays, woman's rights, and a long list of bigoted and phobic fears.

Every war since WW II has been a senseless, unnecessary killing of American men (and recently women) brought on by misguided politicians who have never risked their lives as solder. We have lost our way. No, I'm not proud of today's America.

A few days ago, a Lowe's cashier noticed my military discount. She thanked me for my service. I never risked dying, like so many, and I'm ashamed to accept the thanks, but I say, "Thank you, I'm lucky; I'm a *survivor*."

CHAPTER 73

VETERANS DAY 2019

Since World War II, nearly one hundred thousand solder's lives have been sacrificed, and for what? We should always ask that question, not on this day, but in a cold and sober moment when the flags have been lowered and the bunting removed from public buildings.

We should ask it when we choose our president and members of Congress. 33,686 in Korea, 58,220 in Vietnam, 4,424 in Iraq, and 2,400 in Afghanistan. These men paid the ultimate sacrifice for God and their country, and many did not voluntarily. Yet, these numbers are dwarfed by the number of parents, loved ones, sisters, and brothers who, by their vote and deference to the wisdom of government, allowed it to send their sons to a foreign land to die. And how many were wounded, permanently crippled, and mentally damaged? It's a much, much larger number.

We honor their sacrifice and cloak it with a noble cause: protecting our freedom and making our democracy safe. No mother wants to think she gave her son to geopolitical politics, imagined cold war threats, halted the spread of communism, provided access to oil and other economic benefits, or in the case of Vietnam, saved face from the withdrawal from a no-win, nonsensical war.

I am a veteran of no war. I exited the army before Vietnam. I don't get to wear the "Vietnam Vet" hat, any cap emblazoned with the name of my ship or the military plane I flew. I was never in danger, carried a weapon, and never felt threatened as I drove my English sports car on the back roads of Germany. No one will trace my name on the wall in Washington and say a silent prayer for my anonymous death.

The clerk at Lowe's thanks me for my service, and I mouth a few words about how lucky I am. I am a veteran who didn't die, and I am fortunate. But it's not because my life was protected from harm by the wisdom of our political leaders.

I take pride in that I was willing to make the ultimate sacrifice, unlike our current president, who dodged the draft and disparaged a POW who was captured.

I take pride in the men and women who serve, but I do not take pride in my country for what it has become and for what it has asked from these warriors in the years since WW II.

Shame on us. Shame on those who wrap themselves in our flag while discriminating against those who are not their skin color or their sexual orientation. I didn't join the Army for them. We are better than this, but I fear moving to that better place at eighty years of age will not be in my lifetime.

CHAPTER 74

COLLECTION: POLITICS

CHAPTER 75

PRESIDENT TRUMPKE

With apologies to West Side Story

Dear president Trumpke, we're down on our knees
'Cause no one wants a POTUS with a mental disease
It ain't just a problem you're miss understood
Deep down inside, you're no good

Your no good, your no good
Your no earthly good
Like the best of you is no damn good

Gee, president Trumpke, we're very upset.
You always say something that makes us regret
Electing a person whose IQ is small
Destroying the country, oceans and all
The trouble is you're lazy.
The trouble is you drink
The trouble is you don't know how to think
Trumke, we've got problems everywhere
Our country is in tatters, and you don't seem to care.

Your no good, your no good
Your no earthly good
Like the best of you is no damn good

We're disturbed you like the Putin.
We think you have this crush.
He'll build you a tower, and you'll thank him very much
For Ivanka's spa and all that extra dough
It's the art of the deal; who says he is our foe
Obama made you angry; we get that right away
His liberal agenda never saved the day
So one by one, you'll kill his institutions
But no one will hold you for any better solutions

Your no good, your no good
Your no earthly good
Like the best of you is no damn good

President Trumke, the wall was never been needed.
But it'll keep you in 2020 from ever being defeated
The rapist and drug lords will fall off their ladders
And you'll tell all that country that's all that matters
When Mueller is done, you'll claim there was no collusion
Your republican base will have the same conclusion
But it won't be the stars and stripes; it'll be the bars and stripes
That will end this country's fatal delusion
That a Trumke like you is the solution.

Your no good, your no good
Your no earthly good
Like the best of you is no damn good
So, gee, president Trumke, Trump you.

CHAPTER 76

REPUBLICAN NICENE CREED

We believe in one Trump, the "Donald."
Maker of casinos and towers
And much that is seen and unseen.
We believe in one candidate, Donald Trump,
The wealthy son of Fred Trump
Eternally praised by his father
Trump from Trump, wealth from wealth
Actual billionaire from true greed
Self-made and not elected.
Through him, towers were built.
For us and our gambling addiction
He came down an escalator
With the power of electricity
To become a candidate to close the borders
And export the aliens
For our sake, he debated the unworthy
He suffered under Megan Kelly
And was scorned for his views
But on the next day, he rose to the top of the polls
And ascended to the electable status

He will be seated center stage in the next debate
He will come again in glory to be our next president
And prove the democrats wrong
And help us Make America Great Again
AMEN

CHAPTER 77

FLORIDA SANTA LEGISLATION

CNN BREAKING NEWS:

Republicans in the Florida state legislature, and several other "red" states in the south, have proposed a new "kinder registration" requirement for visits to see Santa Claus.

Children must present proper identification to meet with Santa. Age restrictions and evidence of appropriate behavior must be certified by this identification. Santa monitors are allowed to be present to ensure compliance and report any violations of this new law.

The days permitted to make visits and the operating hours have been shortened, especially in areas of the state where low economic potential would render such visits unrewarding.

"We want to keep all children free of unrealistic expectations being set by visits to fake Santas." A state-issued Santa license must be on display at all times.

This new law will regulate and bring order to the current unfettered access to Santa help that has yet to be vetted. It is for our children's protection and to eliminate wholesale fraud's current status.

CHAPTER 78

COLLECTION: EVERYTHING ELSE

CHAPTER 79

THE BEST WAY
TO TELL

We were standing next to two gorgeous women, giving them the eye. I was ready to make a move when my buddy pulled me aside.

He says, "You wanna know how I tell? OK, the first thing I look for is moisture. It's subtle. Look in the corner of the eyes, near the mouth, the nape of the neck, or under Adam's apple. If it's a hot day, look for perspiration in the armpits; do you get the idea? Be careful, some of the newer models have moisture injection at critical locations, so it's easy to be thrown off.

Another thing. If you can get close enough, listen for a soft whirr when a leg or arm extension is made. The motors are buried inside and are highly soundproofed, but if the room is quiet or you've run into one of the cheaper models, it's a dead giveaway.

And there's another way someone told me about; he says it's foolproof. Engage in casual chitchat, and then suddenly ask a highly technical but nonsensical question. Like this:

'You live nearby?'
'

Sure, I live on Elm Street, near the firehouse.'
'

Have you noticed a rapid de-fluxing near the boundary of the entropy expansion system?'

"It's like they freeze for a moment; 'cause their motor functions are a lower priority to voice recognition and data processing. You can tell that everything is stopped. It'll take a few seconds, actually too many seconds—it'll seem awkward—while they sort out the nonsense. Then you'll get a laugh, or they give a quizzical expression. But it's too late, and it's a giveaway.

And if you meet one at a bar, don't waste your time. Despite all the jokes, it's just not going to work. It's nice to know that science hasn't perfected everything. There's nothing down there. If you can look around—I can't imagine how that would happen—you'll probably see the umbilical connector. I mean, where else would they put it?"

He continued, "This is important: don't try to kiss one or do anything else involving the mouth. It's dangerous. Please don't ask me how I know. There are stories…okay, I know there are still a few things you could do, but if it were me, I'd keep looking for the 'real deal.' Maybe in a few years—there's a lot of research money being invested in that—but not now.

I know all this doesn't sound very easy, but trust me, once you can read the signs, you'll spend much less time with the droids and more time with real chicks. Who knows, maybe your love life will improve."

We both turned at the same time toward the two women; they were oddly silent.

"

Yep," he says, "another thing, droids don't talk to each other."

CHAPTER 80

CONFESSIONS OF A SEVENTY-SOMETHING BICYCLIST

I belong to a bicycle club and, with friends, ride 2 to 3 times a week on rides that range between 30 and 50 miles, but I also have an affinity and a connection to anyone I see in full bike regalia. In a store or restaurant, I resist the urge (or not) to ask about their ride, where they're going, or what bike they are riding. On the highway, I give them a wide berth because I know what it's like to be brushed by a passing car, and I wouldn't say I like it. We have an unspoken but instant camaraderie based on individual bike riding experiences that are mutually understood but not shared. Those experiences are profoundly personal and cut to the core of how we believe our lives should be lived and the intimate relationship we have established with our bodies.

I am addicted to bicycle riding and need a bike "fix" regularly. Why, even after a challenging ride, do I feel this way? Is it seeing my friends again and registering that I'm still riding and healthy? Is it being outdoors and experiencing our beautiful environment at a pace I can appreciate? Is it the satisfaction of riding a fantastic machine that has evolved to be a near-perfection translation of my leg rotations into highway miles? Is it the knowledge that I have the strength to do it at my age? Is it a brain chemical that floods my body after a hill is climbed or a ride is completed? Yes, it is all those things, yet it is something more personal and something I never talk about or share.

Like all severe bicycle riders, I have established a close relationship with my physical body. Over time, a bicyclist (or any person doing physically demanding cardiovascular activity) arrives at a point where his mind and body are dancing, treading the fine line between exhaustion and pure physical pleasure. We learn to do this respectfully, so the experience is balanced. The body rewards the mind with its best performance, and the mind acts as a good steward, not demanding more than the body can give. As in horse and rider, the two become one moving entity at that moment.

On any given ride, I frequently operate close to the limit of my body's performance. Heart. Lungs and muscles only have so much to offer, and I have learned to monitor them to know when those limits have been reached. I also know when I can go into overload, and when the top of the hill is in sight, I dig deeper for something my body and I both know is unsustainable. Surprisingly, I have become comfortable doing this dance and know that my transgressions of pride or vanity will be forgiven at the top of the hill.

I also believe (or want to believe) that I have found a way to slow down my body's aging. I look for and take comfort in the visible signs that it's working. Maybe it is a blood pressure that's lower than usual or a resting pulse in the fifties. Maybe it's my unrevealed smile when the doctor says, "you must be doing something right." Or, it could be something I'm less proud of and don't want to admit, that I beat you to the top of the hill or have my bike in the car when you're just riding into the parking lot. That's why I control my breathing when I join the group at the top of the hill and pretend my chain has come off when I need a rest. It's a kind of smugness and vanity that I fight but doesn't always win.

I know that ultimately, no matter how many riders are with me or whether I'm in the front or the back, I ride alone in an intimate, zen-like world of my mind and body. The cadence, the stroking, and the exertion transport me to a personal experience I don't share.

And yet, we are alike. I may only know your first name, but I know something about you that will bring you here for the next ride, maybe to the top of the hill ahead of me.

CHAPTER 81

BODY LOVE HATE

We have a love-hate relationship with our bodies, and it's not the mirror returning a less Hollywood-perfect image, although, for many, that may be reason enough. No, it's the failures of our flesh that, mistakenly, seem to be entirely out of our control. We love a body that can swim a length in the pool, ride a bicycle, or respond to a lover's caress, but we hate the body that pauses in a flight of stairs, sags, and droops beyond concealment, or worse, and for no apparent reason, gets ill. We curse the imperfect vessel that weakly transports our brain around the planet and delivers our soul too soon to heaven.

It's not always that way. Children represent the complete fusion of mind and body. A child will skip and leap for no apparent reason in a celebration of mind and body that has no separation. We start our journey in life with that perfect harmony, and yet, somewhere along the way, we begin to live more in mind and less in the body. The body, being the wonderful instrument it is, cooperates with this priority and delivers everything the mind wants with little complaint.

It does that beyond reason, and for as long as it can until one day, it delivers less than we want, and we are disappointed. Strangely, we are surprised by this failure and may even feel anger or hate toward it. We search for answers to reinforce the idea that we are the innocent victim of a flawed body. Was it our family genes, a childhood fall at the skating rink, a spray of toxic fumes as we walked by an industrial plant, or bad luck?

In a moment of self-honesty, we may also ask: was it neglect, of not paying attention to its health, that is to blame? Have I been a good body-Stewart? It's an opportunity for reflection on what we have been eating and drinking, what exercise we have elected to do or not, and whether we have listened to the small signals the body delivers after a period of excess or neglect.

What does a mind know about a body? Sadly, the answer is often less than necessary to lead a long and healthy life. Our cultural model of the body, especially in the United States, is that of a motorcar. It needs fuel and occasional maintenance but little else. It can be driven as much as you want and never needs rest time in the garage. Ironically, we know more about caring for our cars than our bodies.

Unless educated, the mind has no concern for the quality or purity of our food or the value of exercise and good sleep. There needs to be more reinforcement for these ideas in mainstream American life. And religion, for the most part, views the body as an imperfect vessel for the soul. We are encouraged to love God, but in an unspoken way, discouraged from the sin of worshiping our bodies by paying attention to worldly things such as nutrition and exercise. Is it "worshipping" or honoring and respecting the body? We are left to decide that question on our own.

"Health nuts" at the fringes of society advocate blenderized concoctions of raw vegetables as the proper diet. Deeply sculptured men or woman mount stone age-looking medieval torture instruments for exercise. It's easy to tune them out. As for training, sports have been co-opted by professional athletes on television screens that we watch passively from our couches. We could never do that. Looking for an easy solution to our body issues, we turn to the pharmaceutical industry for a pill that will reduce blood pressure, lower cholesterol, take off unwanted pounds, and even produce an erection should we get in the mood for sex.

The journey back to the child-like love of the body is none of the above. There is no formula to be followed. Like so many things in life, it starts with the knowledge that the body, not just the mind, needs to be fed good food. It also begins with an act of faith that the reward for the journey back to mind *and* body health will be more joyful than anyone can fully articulate. The rest of the story—what to eat, how to exercise—will unfold before you. It could start today.

CHAPTER 82

DIGNITY

Dignity is our most significant personal treasure. It is the sum of all our parts: our faith, values, and love for all things. When we are "nice," we are not risking our dignity; we risk time poorly spent and the opportunity to be with someone who will appreciate and respect who we are. No one can diminish our dignity unless we put it on the line to be debated or analyzed. If someone in your life seeks to diminish you with the mistaken belief that it will enhance them, run as fast as you can from that person ... to someone who appreciates who you are. Be nice to that person; it's what we are here for. Life is short, and time poorly spent can never be recovered.

Dignity is our most significant personal treasure. It is the sum of all our parts: our faith, values, and love for all things. When we are "nice," we are not risking our dignity; we are risking time poorly spent and the opportunity to be with someone who will better appreciate and respect who we are. No one can diminish our dignity unless we put it on the line to be debated or analyzed. If someone in your life seeks to diminish you with the mistaken belief that it will enhance them, run as fast as you can from that person to someone who appreciates who you are. Be nice to that person; it's what we are here for. Life is short, and time poorly spent can never be recovered.

CHAPTER 83

DAMN YOU, MARK ZUCKERBERG

Confession of a Facebook Supplicant

I constantly check my FaceBook page to see if you've posted something new about yourself. Lunch? Maybe you're checking in at a restaurant? I want to be the first to like your new adventure, no matter how personal or banal your post may be. And I will comment, too. I'll try to be witty, turn a phrase, join the chorus of other supplicants who follow your every move, and hope you have a nice lunch.

I've learned so much about you; you have been willing to share everything—the time you got a traffic ticket for no good reason. It made me mad too. I stay close to my computer, knowing I have to be diligent. If I'm at the bottom of a scrolling list of comments, you may not see mine, and be assured that I follow your every move. You may lose interest and block me, or worse, unfriend me. Losing a friend, even a FaceBook "friend," hurts. And I have so much invested in our relationship.

We are friends, aren't we? Facebook "friends." I remember the day you accepted my invitation. I felt connected to you and you to me. Or are we? I notice you never respond to anything I post. You have so many friends; you must be busy. Or maybe I'm not posting anything interesting? Maybe my post about income inequality was not aligned with your views, and you hate politics? My posts may be a message in the bottle, never to land on *any* digital shore.

But I will never know for sure. Facebook offers no tools to determine if a friend sees my posts. Friends can swoop in any time, look at my wall, post a pithy remark, and then escape to their better-liked friends. I am the fisherman on the bank. One tiny nibble, and I will be there all day, waiting. But there is a way. I will post a "What's on your mind, William" that I have been diagnosed with stage 4 and have only months to live. That will be a test. Hello, are you out there? I'm dying! Silence. Who, except your worried sister, will take the bait and offer condolences ("likes" would not be appropriate in this instance)? Who will immediately set my Facebook flag blazing? Possibly no one, and finding that out will be hurtful.

It was a simple idea: a web page connects college friends to share information. The brainchild of a few young men at Harvard who learned to program the new phenomenon, the internet. It was easy to do. But it had a dark side, the shameless dissection of girls. Big breasts? An easy lay? It was a ranking system for choosing a college date. It caught on, and ownership was fought over.

The application, called "The Facebook," moved from Harvard to Palo Alto and soon spread across the land, like kudzu, to "ordinary" people like you and me. It was recast to fit all markets and was upgraded over and over. Monetization was enviable; it soon became a money-printing machine. At first, no one said the words, but the concept of social media was born.

What could go wrong? A lot can go wrong, and it has. It started with college girls having hurt feelings, and now it's impacting geopolitical politics and national elections. And there's more. As with any innovation, there are unintended consequences. The pernicious nature of man's greed, the easy access to powerful tools to influence public opinion, and the force that lurks in all of us—the desire to be liked—have all conspired to take FB to the dark side. For good or bad, the impact of FB on our lives is indelible and often hurtful. And not talk about the effect on your self-esteem, your feeling of being disconnected, disconnected, unnoticed, and unliked.

But I have it figured out. I'm a FaceBook supplicant, and it's got to stop. It's time to resign from the FaceBook fan club. Time to pull the plug on Mark Zuckerman. I'm going to post this essay on FaceBook and go out in a blaze of glory ... if anyone sees it.

CHAPTER 84

GERALDINE IS OVERWEIGHT AND BLACK

She stood cutting slices of melon for the weekend shoppers to sample. COSCO was abuzz with carts and hungry shoppers, queuing for handouts and causing traffic jams at every intersection. L oblivious to others, many grazers stopped and eyed the proffered tray for the largest samples.

The parade of carts created a backup, not for those who wanted to get around, but for those waiting to get their fair share of the free food. Kids in carts were fed from the tiny cups, making it appear like a parody of a scene from Alice in Wonderland. It put me in a bad mood.

These folks could fill up their jumbo carts to the groaning point and never flinch at the cost presented at the register. Some used flatbed carts and carefully stacked their purchases until it looked like a pallet of relief cargo, ready to be bailed and airlifted to the Congo. Yet here they were, in polite lines, begging for small bits of melon from Geraldine. Their journey from station to station was a mobile smorgasbord.

Geraldine, a smile on her face, her grey wig neatly coiffured, her plastic gloved hands rapidly filling the bowels, wasn't hired to think about such things; she was hired to cull from the large bins of fruit the sweetest, ripest melons— lulling you into thinking they were all that way. But she knew better; that was her secret, her bit of power over the silent parade of beggars who rarely looked at her or thanked her.

I pushed my cart into an empty aisle and left the store. I decided to come back another day when it's only the retirees, like me, in the store.

Monday morning, when COSCO raised the chain curtain at the front door (it reminded me of a feed yard gate), I made a beeline for the fresh vegetables area, and luckily, Gladys was working that day. She was at her station on the same activity as before, cutting fresh melon into samples.

I stopped at the large bin, did my best to smell, thump my way to a good choice, and then took it to her. "What do you think about this one?" I said.

She took her time sizing up my choice, then asked me when I would eat it.

"Soon, maybe tonight."

She had a severe look and explained that my choice might not be edible for several days. She took one from the small pile she had assembled and handed it to me. "Take this one; it's ready right now."

We talked for a while about how to choose a good melon. She and I were alone; no carts were queuing, and she took her time, passing on all her secrets. It reached a point when I could have quickly thanked her and walked away, but instead, I spoke my name and extended my hand. She pulled off her glove and gave me hers,

"I'm Geraldine."

Until then, I didn't know her name; no food sample people wore name tags. They were invisible, human food dispensing "machines" for the cart-people who passed by.

In the conversation that followed, and after suggesting that she was my age, I asked why she was not retired. I learned that she was working to earn money for her grandson, to help put him through junior college. I was ashamed I had asked the question that way—it seemed arrogant of me—but she took no offense and explained that it would take a few years, and she was happy to do it. He was a good kid.

As I was leaving, I asked her why she had given away all her secrets to me or others. Might someone else, armed with her knowledge, take her job?

She smiled, "Honey, do you think any of these white folks want to cut Mellon pieces in COSTCO?"

Again, she was chipping away at my arrogance, teaching me something about humility . . . and the way the world worked.

I want to say that from that day forward, she and I were fast friends; it didn't work that way—another lesson I had to learn. I needed to earn her friendship, and it came slowly as I stopped by her station, mentioned her name, and smiled. At first, she returned my smile hesitantly and faintly. Then, over several months, I started to hear, "Good to see you." "Thanks for stopping by." and "My grandson is doing well at school."

Several days ago, I went to COSTCO for a Mellon (no surprise, I'm now addicted to Mellon) and for other bulk purchases. Geraldine was not handing out samples; she had been promoted to the position at the door, checking for COSTCO cards. I was happy for her.

Missing my contact with her, I paid for my purchases and circled back to the entrance.

"What about this, Geraldine? Is this ripe?" I handed her my melon.

She smiled. We both knew it was over-the-top ripe, verging on a state of mushiness that spoils the enjoyment, even if the taste is still there. It's a risk that sometimes pays off, sometimes not.

"Take it back, honey; get a better one."

"No, I'll cut this part off."

Spontaneously, Geraldine placed her around my waist, and I put mine around her. We hugged, in a way player and coach would do, side by side. It lasted a long time; customers with unchecked cards were streaming by.

I don't know what else we said. It's a blur. What I do know is that there are holy people who walk among us, often invisible, who live lives that can teach us something vital if we are open to the possibility that such learning can occur anywhere, as with Geraldine, with her beatific smile, dispensing food samples at COSTCO.

CHAPTER 85

SHOULD I GOOGLE OR WIKIE?

"I'm swimming in a sea of information, at risk of drowning in the thing I love most."

My youthful arrogance moved me to want to know everything as if that were possible. As a young engineer, I razor-bladed articles from technical journals and filed them in folders to be reviewed and categorized later. I spent time in the company library (what is that?) at the Xerox machine, sliding the warm information into my briefcase for the unlikely possibility of reading it later.

A "Google" search was 3-4 books spread out on the library table and trips back and forth to the stacks for more. It was getting to know the reference librarian on a first-name basis. It was a Sherlock Homes challenge, sleuthing the information to avoid lousy evidence, the useless citation, and the book that needed requisitioning from another library (I'll call you when it comes in).

Days later, sitting at my desk, replete with a telephone (by extension), a wooden "IN" box, and a large ink blotter, and with the definitive article in my hand, I highlighted the "real" information I needed to know. Another folder was produced and labeled to show that it was "THE" folder.

My engineering journal, issued and owned by the company, had blank numbered pages and a "witnessed and understood" footnote with space for two signatures on each page. It became the sacred ground to transcribe important information from my collection of important folders, to become the basis to dream, aspire, and conjure information that would inch man's knowledge forward. If my effort appeared new or clever, a colleague would be called to add his signature next to mine. The pages would be Xeroxed and passed around, maybe to the patent department, and later framed in precise language for an article in a technical journal (to be Xeroxed by someone in another company).

It's 2010, and now retired from the world of engineering but still have my young man's thirst to know everything; I sit in front of my iMac with a Google and Wikipedia page open. The mountains of Xerox copies and old journals have been vanquished to live their remaining existence under 10 feet of landfill or recycled into mindless paper napkins at Mcdonald's.

Technology has taken me to this heavily laden table of knowledge, but strangely, I face the same dilemma. A Google search (being careful of the search criteria) serves up thousands of hits. Where to now? Google engineers and programmers have decided which references are presented first, based on an algorithm that will remain forever secret. How is that different from the once-revered reference librarian? I have the same challenge of culling accurate information from digital flotsam and jetsam. I save the reference or, fearing its later disappearance, the document in a folder named "Essential Knowledge" on my hard drive.

Will I later visit that folder and take time to read the article or be content to know that if I need the information, it's in my folder, not Goggle's? The sea of knowledge is so vast that my now-tempered arrogance admits I need to pull back, to give up knowing (or where to look for) how many pounds of enriched uranium was used in "Big Boy." Why not leave this world with the satisfaction of knowing a few things very well? It's the stock and trade on the talk show circuit. "Welcome, Mr. Watson. Let's hear everything about Canadian geese migrations."

I could learn that or make a start. Should I Goggle or Wikie?

CHAPTER 86

SEVENTY YEARS OF ROLLER SKATING

A GOOGLE search will flood your hard drive with everything you want to know about "roller skating," when it was invented in 1735, and then later, in 1863, when skates became four wheels arranged like the car's wheels (we call them quads now), and facts and figures about its spread across America and its subsequent decline, starting in the seventies and eighties. With some gaps for marriage, child raising, and work, I have been skiing since 1952. The latest gap, about six years, might have ended my skating career had I not moved to the Asheville area and discovered a local skiing group. My mind remembers that artful, sure-footed, fast skater, but my body is playing catchup, albeit slowly.

Skating for fun and recreation as a national pastime passed its peak long ago, but it has never gone away and still exists as a competitive sport and a fun activity for folks like us (Asheville Roller Skate Club). Few roller rinks still exist. They are a shaky investment, at best. I skated in the last available rink in San Jose, CA; it closed six years ago. Internet aside, the oldest skater you may run into at Carrier Park who has any personal knowledge of how it all began .... is me.

My skating history went back to the fifties and started with sidewalk skating in clamp-on skates with metal wheels. They were not fun. The clamp on the skate needed a sturdy shoe (which I didn't have) and had leather straps that quickly became painful. A skate key (for the clamping) hung around my neck with a shoestring. A glide lasted about three feet. It's no surprise rink skating soon followed, but in my small town, it was not a fancy building; it was the Bingo hall with the tables removed (but returned for Saturday night Bingo). With organ music blaring, there were only three kinds of skating: skate-dancing with a partner, couples skating with your hands intercrossed, and free skating (or all-skate). That was my only choice as I watched from the sidelines couples doing the two-step, waltz, fourteen-step, toe spins, and routines designed for competition.

No plastic uppers, every skate, no matter how inexpensive, had a leather boot. I skated in my sister's hand-me-down white skates (it never occurred to me to dye them black) with narrow fiber (called composition) wheels with loose ball bearings that fell out if you took them apart. My sisters learned skate-dancing and had wooden wheels that were wider than mine, and used sealed ball bearings. They were called precision skates.

Fast forward 60 years, and the mechanics of my skates at Carrier Park look precisely the same as they did in 1952. The plates, trucks, kingpins, and so on are the same. Wheels are better, made of polyurethane, and almost everyone has sealed ball bearings. And with a nod to progress ... or my cheapness, my boots are plastic.

Skating is not for everyone, but for those who grew up skating or found skating somewhere along the way, the ridiculous idea of mounting wheels on your shoes is a pathway to fun, meeting people, and living a fuller life.

CHAPTER 87

MY CAT LOVER

Every morning, or almost every morning—he gets to decide—Angelo jumps up in my lap for his "pets." I have to signal my readiness by sitting quietly on the couch with my legs extended to the coffee table, forming a cat bed. Once settled, he makes no effort to show his appreciation and waits patiently until I scratch under his neck or finds that perfect spot that triggers his purring. Bingo! I've found a way to keep him while I enjoy my hot tea and think about my day ahead. He's purring, and I'm slurping; two happy souls are caught frozen, leaving the world like space travelers.

At some unpredictable moment, a tipping point is reached. He's still purring, but I know it won't last. I try harder to find a new spot to rub, trying not to signal that I'm desperate to keep him with me longer. But it's to no avail. Like a pickup date on Saturday night, he's had his way with me, and he looks up and abruptly leaves our embrace.

Now I know how a woman must feel as I watch him run to his bowl and eat heartily, feeding his other needs with nothing like a thank-you.

CHAPTER 88

I MAY BE TOO BUSY VOLUNTEERING TO RIDE NEXT YEAR'S CENTURY

Riding a century bicycle ride was never on my "bucket list," but it seemed overdue, especially as I approach a time when I know it won't be an option in the rest home. Having ridden the Tuesday Loop Ride regularly, not to mention several of Andy's meandering rides in lovely neighborhoods and compacted dirt, I felt I was up to the challenge. I also attended the early LDT rides until the mileage and hill climbing numbers damaged my willingness to travel to the start/finish. Still, I thought I could 'tough it out" for the few extra miles required for a metric century.

But hill climbing was another matter. I asked a friend if Redwood Gulch Road was worse than Pierce. Yes. Worse than Mount Charlie? Yes. Worse than Parker Ranch or Peach Hill? Yes, yes. I had run out of personal experience and felt edgy enough to rush home, Google Map Redwood Gulch Road, and turn on street view. It didn't look that bad! The magic of computer surrogate travel and 3D to 2D mapping made it look like a pleasant, tree-lined country road. Maybe I could take my granddaughter there for a Sunday walk?

A few glasses of red wine the night before helped me believe that 6,000 feet of climbing were only a matter of digging a little deeper. The next day, armed with a breakfast of Trader Joe waffles slathered with honey and peanut butter, I flew up Foothill Expressway, then Stevens Canyon Road, to the beginning of Redwood Gulch Road. It was going to be one of those so-called "chain-less" days… or so I thought.

Shifting into my "granny" gear and taking a deep breath, the road was steeper than I imagined. I felt like a marine standing at the base of Mount Suribachi on Iwo Jima. And how did they keep the asphalt paving machine from careening down the hill to the spot where I was now standing?

Soon my "fresh legs," waffles, and help from "granny" gave way to taking frequent water breaks. It's well known that for safety, a rider on a steep hill should stop to rehydrate frequently. At the risk of draining my water bottle, after a while, I was forced to take bike pushing breaks. I was glad to be wearing my Illinois bike club shirt; passing riders would know I deserved to be cut some slack as a flat-rider. The torture was soon over, and as luck would have it, I was actually on my bike when I caught up with my friends.

The middle part of the Century is a blur of more climbing and more climbing, and then a magnificent descent on Alpine Road. This roadside panorama is everything California has to offer, and keeping my eyes on the road ahead was hard. Such beauty could only be tarnished by the realization that every foot of descent would have to be repaid later in the ride. I took comfort that the reputation for good food at the La Honda Center would often refill my gas tank.

After lunch, the Tunitas Creek Road climb back to Skyline Boulevard was not avoided. As far as I know, there is no secret tunnel back to Woodside Road. Tunitas is like a sadistic lover, beckoning you further and further with a gentile climb, and when it's too late to turn around, raising the ante with miles of twist-and-turn climbing. Most riders would agree it's a modest climb, but at this point (unknown to me), I had severely depleted my electrolytes and was cramping out. My salt-encrusted cyclo-computer, now mostly unreadable, should have been a clue. With miles to go to the flat portion (flat means less climbing, but climbing nevertheless), I was again alternatively pushing and riding my bicycle. It's incredible how easy it is to push an all-carbon, 27-speed road bike. As time went on, it occurred to me that I was pushing the same model bike that Lance Armstrong used some years back to win the Tour de France. And then, it may have been a mirage, but I swear an angel that looked like our club president stopped to feed me salt capsules and gooey stuff and followed me to the top of the hill.

Back to Skyline, the rest of the ride is about gravity, a biker's best friend. Like a horse to the barn, I flew down Kings Mountain Road and soon to the Stanford Blood Center. Somewhere on the last leg of the ride, as the cramping and pain became a memory, I made a mental note to myself: stop being cheap and get a "32" on the back; you're not young or even middle-aged anymore.

It also occurred to me that riding the century was selfish; I should be volunteering on Sunday (not just Saturday). I may make this sacrifice next year. And maybe, if I keep the date a secret, my wife may schedule a trip-of-a-lifetime, with a sizeable non-refundable deposit, that "accidentally" falls on the exact date of the Sequoia Century 2013.

CHAPTER 89

ODE TO BETSY

I run to Betsy's bright light, like a little boy chasing a firefly in the woods of Pennsylvania, but she's gone. I want to capture her and spend time in her light, discussing books, philosophers, paintings, and the fast-approaching end of our lives. But like the firefly, she's moved on. Fireflies are like that. Never one place, never one light. She was never risking the capture and the confines of a mason jar or a life not free.

Yet here I am, waiting by the woods for another night, another opportunity, cursing her elusive nature and in awe of the gifts of her light. Those fleeting moments bring me back, time after time, drawn to the intoxication of possibility while accepting the ephemeral nature of her world. Little boys and older men never change and never stop wanting something brilliant to light their dull lives.

Shine on, Betsy, don't stop flying. Don't let gravity or the pull of open arms bring you down to this earth. That's not you. The night sky needs your light; we all do.

CHAPTER 90

SEVEN REASON WHY OPRA DOESN'T RETURN YOUR CALLS

You've always wanted to write. That thought has been tucked in your mind for years while you earned a living, raised kids, and nurtured your engineering career until now, retired; you have the time to fulfill your dream: publishing a novel.

You never considered yourself a "reader." A few books were purchased at the airport to pass the time on an extended business flight, yes, but not serious literature, not since college. You remember those days, reading "Catcher in the Rye" and thinking you could have written that. "I have more pimples than Holden Caulfield." That's what you told yourself then, feeling smug with the humor and vowing to use the line in your first novel. And now that opportunity has come.

It can't be that difficult to write a novel. You have a story; we all do. And lately, you've become more sensitive, someone who could write about deep feelings and feel comfortable sharing long-held yearnings and secret desires. Sometimes those feelings unexpectedly well up, a flood of tears and memory of all that childhood pain you've never shared, let alone put to paper. Well, now you can.

It was hard at first, staring at the blank computer screen and waiting for the words. No dialogue came, so you just started talking to the page about your early life. You told about jobs your grandfather had, about the crazy uncle who filled his basement with wet concrete that set before he could level it. Gradually characters appeared and started speaking. Soon you were writing every morning and then walking around in a daze of dialogue and thought the rest of the day. When it was done, you liked what you had written. It was pretty good. It might need a few tweaks here or there and some minor re-writing, but it was your story, and soon the shelves at Borders would be stocked and re-stocked with your novel.

You rush to Kinkos to make copies. Your lucky friends and relatives would be the first to read your novel. You would soon hear their amazement and amazement that you could write so well. When the clerk at Kinkos told you how much it would cost, you were shocked and immediately shortened the list of reviewers. Some would have to wait and read it in the published form.

The cost of mailing was another shock, but the copies went out, and you waited for the expected praise. And you waited. Gradually, after prodding and appeals to family loyalty, the verdict came in that your first, maybe last, the novel was not worthy of publication. It was a shock, something heavy and final, extinguishing your voice and your dream to be a published novelist. You're not sure if you will write again. Life is short, and you realize that your story has been told, albeit in the wrong way, and you no longer feel the need to say more.

In case you change your mind and decide to write another novel, you assemble a list of seven indicators that would trumpet the inadequacy of your effort:

Your reviewer appears to be stalled, so you tell him to keep reading because "it gets better."

You realize that mention of your novel has joined with the story about the time your father was arrested for shoplifting as a topic never to be discussed by the family.

When your best friend hasn't finished your novel and has time to remodel her house and plant a garden.

When you hear that something your character did was "unbelievable," you respond by saying it *is* believable because you did that.

When you hear that your friend does not like your main character and realize that, as a consequence, she may not like you.

When you hear that the reader likes one of your supporting characters "better" and wants to read more about him.

When your reviewer refuses to acknowledge your draft as a novel (the "N" word) and refers to it as a "start" or "first effort," she encourages you to take writing courses and join a writing group.

CHAPTER 91

HOW TO PUBLISH A GREAT NOVEL

While maintaining your anonymity.

First, pick a catchy book title and Google it to ensure it's not already published. Then print a title page. Use a large font size for the title and a smaller size for the author's name directly below. Use your name—no one in the literary world or anywhere else, except your immediate family, knows you exist. A pseudonym is unnecessary and redundant.

Tape the title page on the wall above your computer and immediately start Googling and exploring Wikipedia for relevant content. Skim the articles and save all the URL references in a " Research folder."

Spend a short time reflecting on whether anything in your past life relates to the title. Don't fret if nothing comes to mind.

Now it's time to start writing. Find your best time. Maybe it's early in the morning after your second cup of coffee but before the contentment and satiation of breakfast stifle your creativity. The first page is essential, so start with catchy phrasing and early-in-the-work ironic twists. Don't be afraid to open a well-liked novel and adapt its first-page format. If it was a dark and stormy night, dare to write that.

Soon, after a few pages of "warming up the creative engine," you will have characters that move and speak, and some plot will emerge. Hint: hold back early plot resolutions; save them for the end of the book. Before each writing day, use Google maps and street view to establish location information. Google again for supporting content like restaurant menus, wine selection, etc. Use actual names of companies and search Yelp for information about them—it's unlikely they will care (or know), and it will lend authenticity. For example, if you're writing about a young engineer working in China, go to a relevant blog and read what that would be like.

After a few months of writing, it's time to end the book, so kill off, retire, or create a tragic bout with cancer to resolve and dispose of supporting characters. It's almost over. At this point, if you don't know how to end the book, have the protagonist take a walk to a famous bridge on a night, stand at the railing, and say something ambiguous and self-destructive. Refrain from typing "The End." Who knows, a sequel may be in the offing.

Now the fun part. Don't have anyone read your novel; they will only criticize your work out of jealousy and envy. And don't do too much editing, as that will destroy the spontaneity of the writing. As a writer, your spelling and grammar are likely better than most of your readers.

NEXT, please print out your book; it will be a large pile of paper...but you're not done. Now, open a published book, and page-by-page, create your version of acknowledgments, dedication, quotes, publishing information, copyright, ISBN, and so forth. Intersperse numerous pages that restate the book title—all publishers do that. Don't pay $15 for a real ISBN. It's not worth it as no one will check to see if it's authentic.

Finally, pick a name for your publishing company—that's you. It's your chance to be creative. Avoid silly phrases like "Full Press" or Flybynight Press." If you want, pick a symbol from an obscure font on your computer, like wingdings, to be your press icon.

After STAPLES prints and binds your "published" novel, take a copy to your library, and at closing time, remove it from your backpack and carefully place it on a shelf next to a famous work of fiction, like Porknoy's Complaint, by Philip Roth, or any novelist starting with the same last name initial as you.

Wait.

CHAPTER 92

YOUR FRIENDLY SUPERMARKET

We are the envy of the world, our supermarket shelves laden with so much food... and so many choices. Yet we still need to walk the aisles, as our mothers did, and our mother's mother did, pulling items from the shelves and heading to checkout. Lasers and bar codes will quickly have the tally. Our bodies have a count too, but we will not know the "price" until much later.

Imagine a drug dealer who offered vitamins, supplements, and drugs, so you could choose between them or buy some vitamins and some medications. Call it a balanced choice... middle of the road. You decide to have a little fun and a little health.

Our supermarkets are like drug dealers; surprisingly, there is little difference between Safeway and Whole Foods. We push our carts down isles and hope for inspiration, knowledge, and, occasionally, forgiveness. We make hundreds of choices, and as parents, choices for our children who won't have a vote on those choices until they leave home. The federal government offers little assistance. The FDA will guarantee you won't die tonight at the supper table, but next week, next month, or your middle age? Well, that's unclear. With 40% of women and 35% of men classified as obese, the warning bells should go off. But instead, in the market aisle, it's music to shop by... and announcements of "bargains" in the meat department or the bakery, where imitation bread is baked every two hours.

We are offered products with ingredients that have yet to be grown in a garden. Chemicals to make it look attractive to keep it from clumping. And worse, additives that make sure it has a long shelf life, a very long shelf life. It's all about convenience and finding a way to prepare meals quickly and easily. We lead busy lives. Our granite-topped modern kitchens are a place to rip open the plastic bags of instant food. The multi-burner stove is pristine and unused. The oven and microwave are all we need. We are like the folks who will someday travel to Mars. We've already seen it in movies: the bins of plastic bags, some labeled beef stroganoff or spaghetti and meatballs. The 30-second cleanup. And the daily pills that somehow make everything work. Yes, we will survive the seven months it takes to get to Mars. But to old age, maybe not.

Every meal has to have protein, and in our sanctioned ignorance (check out the latest FDA food pyramid), that means meat. We don't say animal flesh; that would be gross. We don't stare at legs and flanks and hooves. Instead, it's all so sanitary and tidy in cellophane-wrapped foam trays. A red light overhead helps, too. And we are never reminded that it took hundreds of thousands of gallons of water to raise the animals now eviscerated and waiting patiently in the cooler and that they ate corn, a grain that starving people around the world could live very well on. The collective pollution from factory farming and animal raising dwarfs any other contribution to climate change. Let's not be reminded of that.

It's been a long day. We make our way to the front of the store with our cart. A twelve-pack of coke is on sale; too good to pass up. It will make out a family smile when they see it. And one last thing, at the checkout counter, the Inquirer Magazine. The amorality of the modern supermarket doesn't stop with the body; the mind is fair game. It says the Feds have the "goods" on Hillary; she will never be president. Maybe John Travolta is gay? And what does Barbara Streisand look like on the beach with no makeup?

A drug dealer is more honest. He knows vitamins won't save you.

CHAPTER 93

TOOLS

Who are you? Look in your toolbox for the answer. At least, that was the wisdom of my youth, growing up in the blue-collar world of western Pennsylvania. Community respect came from a collection of tools and the knowledge of how to use them. It was a matter of pride, and it was expected. Everyone had a screwdriver and a pair of pliers, but someone who could overhaul a Chevy straight-six engine needed much more.

As I looked around at my relatives, it soon became apparent, even from my boyhood perspective, that to be a man, you had to be able to do "something," and the more complicated it was, the more likely you would be placed higher in the family hierarchy. It was always something practical and valuable to your extended family. Maybe you could install hardwood flooring, shingle a roof, or lay a cement block foundation. In our poor rural life, the idea that a stranger could be hired, for example, to wire a house, was an anathema. No one had the money to do that; it was only a last resort. You might have to wait until the weekend, and you may have to offer up some quid-quo-pro, but it would be done.

I watched this happen over and over again. At an early age, my labor contributed to this oasis of self-sufficiency. If I could carry a package of three-tab shingles up a step ladder to the roof or know how much water to mix with the cement and sand (it was an art to mix good "mud") to make the bricklaying go well, I was on my way to learning a more excellent skill that would be needed and appreciated. It started with common sense, as it was called then. Only a "dumb guy" would forget to deglaze the brake drums during a brake job or use sealant on a radiator hose. Taking it to a higher level might come from something you learned at work, at the mill, or watching your brother-in-law tear down a car engine and lay all the parts on the garage floor. Yes, those are the pistons, the camshaft, the journal bearings, the valve guides and lifters, and all the other parts. The oil rings wipe the oil from the cylinder walls; the compression rings differ.

My first exposure to such family expertise was my great-uncle, called "Bunky" by everyone. He sat on his front porch most summer nights, drinking a quart of Old Shay Ale and teasing the kids. "Jaybird, Jaybird, sitting on a pole, wiggle-waggle went his tail, and the shit began to fall." We laughed, and he would then explain how to catch a bird: put salt on his tail. His gruff nature was a game he played with us. His serious side was found In his basement: a collection of hand saws that he kept sharpened and the teeth set with a unique tool. He had a saw for cross-cutting and another for ripping. He had a collection of saws and the knowledge of how to measure a two-by-four to create a stud wall. One-by-twelve sheeting was cut at a 45-degree angle for the exterior walls; plywood hadn't been invented.

This man built our house entirely with hand saws, including cutting back the floor joist around the foundation to make room for a brick facade, correcting a wrong choice that was made earlier. After years we spent living in the foundation of an unfinished house. After work, he would show up at our house-to-be with his collection of saws and labor until dark. He was a flawed man in many ways, but he subscribed, as we all did, to the idea that we were relatives and helped each other. Watching my home being built, hearing "get me more nails," and learning that he meant a ten-penny nail (not an eight-penny) was the beginning of my life-long pleasure received from the smell of freshly cut wood and reward for doing physical work.

In the fifties, every family had a car, not two cars, just "a" car. And it was not very reliable. In those days, cars were a constant drain on finances and patience. They were unreliable and prone to breakdowns and frequent, unavoidable maintenance. Every boy, including me, who aspired to own a car quickly learned a new vocabulary. Every car will need: brake jobs, grease jobs, points and plugs, shocks, tie rods, ball joints, clutch replacement, wheel bearings, a ring job, muffler replacement, and if all those things don't help, a radiator flush and so on. Maybe a total engine overhaul was needed. An excellent job at the steel mill might put a new Chevy in the driveway, but after handing over the keys, the dealer would say, "make a list of all the defects and bring it in." Several years later, the new car smell was barely gone, and brown spots would appear in the fender wells along the trunk line—rust. Cars "rusted-out." You could do nothing except try an after-market undercoating called Ziebarth. The dealer gleefully took your money, put the car on a rack, and spread some goo over the car's underbelly. It barely helped.

Growing up, I never knew any relative who took their car to a shop. A car mechanic's shop. If there were no relatives in the family inventory of skills that could work on a car, it was taken to someone known to be a cheap "shady-tree" mechanic. It was the cost of parts plus some labor; always a guess. But we had Billy Rob, my uncle. He lived next door and had all the tools. How else would a boy of 15 know what a ridge-reamer was, a spinner tool, like an egg beater, to seat the new valves (with valve seating compound), a cylinder ring compressor? And a long list of other specialty tools. He would "mike," use a micrometer, and determine if you needed oversized/undersized crankshaft bearings.

With his help, at age 15, I could do a points and plugs replacement. "Put the car in high gear, push it to rotate the distributor shaft to maximum lift (maximum point opening), then use a feeler gauge to set the gap." Later, he showed me how to use a timing light and rotate the distributor body to set the timing.... so many degrees before the top-dead-center. He explained that it would be too late to fire the combustion mixture when the cylinder reached the top of its travel. The light illuminated a tic mark on the crankshaft pulley. It was pretty simple.

Billy Rob had everyone's respect. His drinking didn't seem to matter that much. It's like the adage, "marry a butcher, and you'll never starve." Today, there are no Billy Robs. And very few shade-tree mechanics. Car repairs are just too sophisticated, and the tools are even more specialized. If there is any good news in this, modern metallurgy has all but eliminated ring and valve jobs. The smoking cars we saw all the time in the past are gone. "Your car is too young to smoke," people would say. Today, it may never take up the habit.

My dad valued tools all his life. They became his legacy for me, his only son. I frequently hear, "when I am gone, I want you to have this." It was a tool of some type, on sale and a good buy, he would say, something, someday, that I would surely need.

I never knew exactly what he did on those river boats, deep in the engine room, below the water line. He would bring the room a canvas bag of tools from his several-month journey down the Mississippi on a tow boat. He would spend several weeks, maybe a month, at home, but I seldom saw any tool taken from the bag to fix something around the house. He had long abdicated his position of a man of the house, and even as a young boy, with his long absences, I learned to paint a room, light the furnace, and fix a light fixture. The other gaps in his life at home, like being a husband, I could never fill, only in the dreams and aspirations of my mother, who wanted me to be a "professional," a man that wore a shirt and ties every day, like her father, but not her husband.

My dad continued to buy tools throughout his life, stashing them in drawers and heavily laden shelves in the garage. Most were never opened; after his death, their packaging still intact, given to Good Will. We know some were never paid for, like the purloined tools from the boat, stamped with HAW for Harold Albert Watson. The store clerks knew to oversee him as he moved among the sale items at SEARS. The line between reality and his private world was never clear, especially after his head injury on a ship at sea. He was a good man and faithful to the family as a provider, but he never found or was offered the right "tool" to make his life better and less sad.

My toolbox? Now late into retirement and someone who doesn't need many tools, I look at my inventory and see an eclectic mix of good and barely usable tools. Given my childhood and reverence for devices I witnessed, you might imagine DeWalt and other high-end tools neatly arranged by size, category, and shape. Not so. My last house remodel was primarily accomplished with Harbor Freight tools, the lowest rung on the tools-for-respect scale. My reasoning for using poor-quality tools while saving thousands and thousands of remodel dollars is not easily explained. Perhaps I still think, "poor?" Maybe I've learned to take the tool out of the equation and work well despite limitations. I will never know and won't be naming any tool in my will when I'm gone. Just like I did with my dad's tools, my sons will take my collection to Good Will.

Looking back at my growing up experience, I realize it prepared me to do many amazing things—build an airplane, remodel a kitchen, build a shed, etc.—and the only tools I needed were the childhood learning of how to do it. In my professional life, I became an engineer, and the tools were never physical; in my private life, I became a man that could do almost anything, and knowledge was the only "tool" that mattered. You can't put that in a will.

CHAPTER 94

YOU DON'T OWN YOUR CAT

After reading Billy Collin's poem "The Revenant."

Papers and pedigree to the contrary, you don't own your cat any more than you can own a summer shower or an ocean breeze. He may agree to be with you in exchange for food and shelter, but it's a bargain you must renew every day. A neighbor's bowl of Eukanuba or an open door may be all it takes for him to move house, grace another chair with his stunning beauty, or sit in their sunny window. Without a thought or regret, he will have you walking the neighborhood, repeatedly crying and calling his name.

It's not a flaw in his design, a pernicious nature, or unbounded arrogance that locks up his heart. No, it's his density to own pride, to have his wives perform the hunt, to sit in the sun, to watch for competitors, and to sleep. We can't take him from the jungle and expect anything else. But we do.

A cat lost at a turnpike rest stop will not spend his remaining life searching for you. It is an accident if he passes your house and you run out to hug him. He wasn't looking for you.

When a cat runs to the door to greet you, don't believe you have been missed. His eyes are on the open door. You better close it quickly, or he will bolt to a new life, only returning if better accommodations cannot be found.

An indoor cat is a caged animal. Unlike a zoo, we live with our captive and imagine a higher relationship. If we are lucky and he jumps onto our lap for affection, it's not love. He needs you to scratch a place he can't reach or take your turn watching for danger. And when he moves away, and your heart goes with him, he's not thinking of you; he's thinking about a cozy spot to take a nap or has seen the flutter of a bird's wing.

When age and a failing kidney place him in the carrier for a last trip to the vet, and when you hold him and look into his eyes for the last time, you are not saying goodbye to your cat. You are saying goodbye to a fellow traveler who has decided to leave you.

CHAPTER 95

ZEN AND THE LOVE OF BICYCLE RIDING

The hill is steeper than I'd thought. I flick the right paddle shifter to move the chain on the rear wheel sprocket to a lower gear, finessing the shift and my pressure on the crank to make it happen without losing too much speed or clanking the gears. I'm starting to go anaerobic; my breathing is shallower, and I'm on the verge of panting. I can feel my leg strength diminishing, and since I'm in the lowest gear, my "Granny" gear, I debate whether I should lower my peddling cadence or try to tough it out.

I can see the crest of the hill ahead, so I decide to move beyond the pain and push harder on the pedals, the way runners do when they near the finish line, reaching for something inside of me that is unsustainable and risky.

This is the place I visit each bike ride on the many steep hills in Northern California. Intuitively, it doesn't make any sense. Why would you push your body to the point of exhaustion repeatedly? Why having experienced that level of pain, would you be willing to share it again and again yet look forward to the next ride with anticipation and excitement?

That answer goes beyond the simple explanation of endorphins the brain releases, creating a sensation of pleasure, ultimately igniting an addiction in the rider, though perhaps a positive one. It dwells in the mystery of the mind-body connection. Over time, the bicyclist (or any person doing physically demanding cardiovascular activity) arrives at a point where his mind and body are dancing, treading the fine line between exhaustion and pure physical pleasure. They learn to do this respectfully, so the experience is balanced. The body rewards the mind with its best performance, and the mind acts as a good steward, not demanding more than the body can give. As in horse and rider, the two become one moving entity at that moment.

At puberty, most people have developed a love-hate relationship with their bodies. Maybe we're not as handsome or beautiful as we wanted to be; perhaps we didn't make the football team, or maybe we have suffered from some disease or disability. Often, a healthy mind resides in a much less-than-perfect vessel.

In our later years, we will probably rattle off a list of afflictions, ranging from allergies to high blood pressure. We imagine ourselves to be victims of the aging process. It is rarely written that we bear, to a greater or lesser part, responsible for many of our old age woes.

It's not surprising that our lifetime of distancing our minds from our bodies leads to neglect and abuse. It doesn't explain every medical condition we encounter, but not challenging our bodies is high on the list of causes of poor health. With society's emphasis on physical appearance, the stress for healthful living is mainly on a diet; exercise is given only a polite nod. Become thin, and for men, go to the gym and bulk up. That's the mantra — if we look good, we feel good!

What needs to be appreciated is that cardiovascular fitness is the beginning and end points of health lasting into old age. Why? When we pursue such fitness, the effort and the necessity to take ownership of our bodies to guide us to a better diet and lifestyle.

Of course, all of this requires diligence. No pill, no TV abductor machine, and no amount of reps on a resistance machine at the gym will get you there. We will be on a bicycle, in a pool, cross-country skiing, or in some exercise that increases our heart rate (doctor's approval required). The surprise I've discovered is the pleasure of hanging out with a body at this new level of health and strength. It is joyful.

I fight the urge to slow down and rest as I reach the top of the hill. It takes some effort, but I keep the peddling cadence up, and by the time I have shifted several times into higher gears, I can already feel my leg strength returning. In another few minutes, the memory of the effort to reach the top of the hill is already fading, and my body is singing again.

There may be a glorious downhill ahead, or there may be yet another hill. It doesn't matter. My mind, my body, and my bicycle are ready.

CHAPTER 96

SHORT STORY: ABBY'S BABY

In 2006 the US population reached 300 million. In the following decades, it increased at a rate greater than expected. Once considered nearly infinite, global coal, gas, and oil resources declined. Energy costs were spiraling. Alternative energy sources are needed to be keeping pace with growth. The government, fearing an economic meltdown and social chaos, has imposed strict measures to halt population growth. Abby and Larry want a baby, but now they need more than sperm and egg; they need a certificate from the government stating that someone has died.

Good.

The waiting room was almost empty, with no pumpkin-bellied women reading BabyCare magazine, looking smug, reminding Abby that she was not pregnant, had no children, and was running out of time.

Abby hated these yearly visits to Dr. Holden, hated the predictable conversation: "Abby, I want to help you, but there is nothing I can do until you get permission."

She sat next to one of the flat-stomached women and waited for the nurse to start the terrible business.

"Right in here, dear, put this on."

"OK"

Abby looked at her body. Pretty good for someone 36. Thirty-six, she had only four more years until forced sterilization. No signs of the ravages of two late-term abortions, both resulting from her false hopes of having gained permission. Her husband, Larry, and Dr. Holden had been angry with her for "jumping the gun."

"Abby, how are you, and how is Larry?"

"He's fine."

"And what about you?"

"Well, it's same-old, same-old."

He looked at her for a long moment as if he were cutting back her skin and muscle to look at an internal organ.

"Abby, I'm worried about you. You know, having a baby is a wonderful thing, but it's not everything. You and Larry can have a good life, and everyone knows bringing another consumer into the world is not what our planet needs."

"Dr. Holden, I want a baby, not a consumer. I know the rules; it's just that I ...."

Abby felt the familiar longing sweep over her body. It was the same feeling she had, day after day when the mothers came to collect their children from the KiddyCare Center where she worked. She wanted her baby. What was so wrong with that? Why couldn't the planet support one more child? It wasn't fair.

Dr. Holden had seen this same expression on her face last year and the years before. He felt sorry for her but was not about to volunteer his aging mother.

"Abby, I'm here; we're all here to help you. If you get permission, I will have the entire hospital staff lined up to make it happen. Now, lean back, and let's see how you are doing."

* *

With one practiced push, Larry lifted his feet and wheeled his desk chair out of his cube and into the hallway. No one was around. It was time to check his bid on e-Auction; if his boss saw him, he would have some explaining to do. The company had quietly installed employee computer usage software, and it had logged that Larry was spending much time on e-Auction. His boss put a note in his employee file, saying that company rules forbid personal computer use. It could get him fired.

Well, he could play that game too. It only took a few lines of code to trap the e-Auction URL and turn it into the one for the company website. As long as his computer screen was not seen, he was now a model employee. What if they installed a camera in the ceiling? He turned the monitor contrast down until he could barely read the e-Auction window on his screen.

The top of the window had an old-fashioned gavel, repetitively hitting a block of wood, surrounded by miniature computers with arms and legs, each holding up a paper bid.

Next, his bid item was represented by an icon-sized version of the government's official Baby Entitlement Document, or BED, overprinted with the date when the seller agreed to go to the nearest government-run Gateway Transition Center to be terminated. Larry and Abby could then use the issued BED document to establish their right to have a baby. Simple — zero population growth.

His bid status, followed by the shipping choices and cost, were summarized at the bottom. For a BED auction, "shipping" was the transportation cost to get the seller to the nearest Gateway Transition Center. The choices for train and bus were grayed out. Larry always checked first-class air, hoping the e-Auction software would note his generosity and raise his bid priority.

Amazingly, Larry was still the highest bidder, and it was less than 24 hours until the close of bidding. Somebody out there wanted to end their life for money. He stopped wondering about why years ago; he and Abby were glad they did.

Who was the jerk that thought up the BED acronym? He and Abby, and all the other childless couples, were the brunt of endless BED jokes, like, "How many BEDs does it take to make a baby?

Answer: one." The furniture companies, unwilling to risk the double meaning, now called their beds "sleepers."

Despite their lack of success, he and Abby had agreed to keep trying, and over the years, their bid money had grown to $100,000. It was a large sum, but always in the past, and he suspected now someone would swoop in at the last second and outbid them. The other choice, e-Auction-Adoption, was hopeless. They had gone through the lengthy process of being pre-qualified, but the bidding was astronomical. Besides, any child in the $100,000 range would probably have hidden genetic defects despite the "clean" DNA report on the bid page.

Larry was startled by his best friend Mark's appearance at his cube entrance.

"Hey Lare, how's your bid on that ancient i-POD? Can you still get batteries for those things?"

It was their coded language, used so that anyone hearing wouldn't know their shared secret about Larry's bidding for a BED; it had been going on for years. Mark never got tired of the "game" and grinned like an oaf. He had every reason to smile; his wealthy parents had included two BEDs among his many wedding gifts. If you have money, you could get anything on the black market.

Since he was still in the bidding, he gave this reply:

"Batteries will be included."

"Hang in there, Lare; say hi to Abby."

Mark left, and the phone rang no sooner than he closed the e-Auction window — management would be happy with his visit to the "company" website. He knew it was Abby.

"Abby, hi."

"Yeah, I knew it was you. How's your day going?"

"That's good to hear. Mark says hello."

"No, I'll be on time tonight."

Abby cut the small talk; I know why you're calling. I'm not sure if I should tell you, but yes, we're still the highest bidder."

Abby, for God's sake, doesn't get your hopes up. You know what can happen. We'll talk more tonight."

"I love you too."

* *

Abby knew Larry was avoiding the subject of their e-Auction bid. She tried to suppress her giddy feeling that this time it was different. She could imagine opening the registered mail and dancing around the room with the BED in her arms, like a paper baby.

They had always been outbid in the past. Larry was keeping something from her. It may have happened already.

"Larry, what about the bid? Are we still the highest?"

"Yes — I can't believe it. We're at $90K, so we have room to go higher. I installed a freeware program that will do it automatically if we need to."

"Oh, Larry, this could be it. It's what I've always wanted."

Abby watched Larry's face caught up in the excitement for a moment, slowly turning back to the old Larry she knew. It was Larry that wanted to run away, wanted to avoid hope, and wanted to be safe with his feelings.

"I can't take this much longer. I know you…we…want a baby, but I'm almost ready to pack it in."

Abby knew this was dangerous ground, but her whole life was teetering.

"Larry, what about your father? He's almost 70 and has complained about his arthritis a lot."

"If dad went to Gateway, it would kill mom. I can't ask him to do that."

"Your mom could go too. Many couples do that. They've had a long and good life. We're just starting ours. Wouldn't they want to carry on the Gilbert name? We could use the sex isolation procedure with your sperm and have a boy. Under the circumstances, I'm sure the government would approve."

Larry got up and started pacing.

"What about *your* mom?" She can't be happy being alone. Your dad Gateway goes for Barbara; now it's her turn to help you. Have you spoken to her?"

Larry was right. Abby had never opened the subject with her mother, thinking that she would already know how much Abby wanted a baby.

"No, but I'll talk it over with my sister tomorrow; we're having lunch."

Suddenly, the air was gone from the room. Abby felt exhausted and sick. Larry was near the breaking point too. And why? She hated the government, the selfish people who had too many children, the planet for not having more oil, and herself for wanting to bring a baby into this kind of world.

"Let's go to bed, Abby; we may get lucky."

"You go; I want to sit here and have a glass of wine."

* *

Anna was six now and in the first grade. It gave Barbara new freedom and, from Abby's perspective, a perfect life.

Seven years ago, dad became terminally ill. After much family discussion and tears, he went to the Gateway center nearby and ended his life, designating the BED to Barbara. Anna was the result. Out of concern for their mother, now alone, they'd agreed to have lunch once a month, usually discussing something about her care.

It was hard getting through lunch, with the small talk and the food Abby barely tasted. When coffee arrived, Abby took a deep breath.

"I want to talk about mom helping me have a baby."

"Christ, Abby, you're talking about Anna's grandmother. What about e-Auction? What about the national lottery for unclaimed BEDs?"

"It's not working. I never win anything; I only have four more years, and it's over. I'm running out of time. Why should you have everything?"

"I don't have everything. Anna is lonely and needs a sister or brother."

"I want to talk to mom and get an agreement."

Barbara folded her napkin, looked the other way for a moment, and then squarely back at Abby.

"I've already talked to mom."

"What?"

"Look, I'm 38. I only have two more years left, less than you. Anna needs a brother or sister; mom knows that. And besides, I've proven that I can have a healthy child. We tested Anna's DNA; it's almost perfect. Your baby would be a complete unknown. Mom's life could be wasted."

Abby couldn't speak. Tears welled up in her eyes as she stared at Barbara. She was a stranger and, now, her enemy.

"What did she say?"

"She's going to think about it."

Her cell phone rang; it was Larry.

"Barbara, I gotta go. It's Larry. It could be important."

Walking out of the restaurant with the phone to her ear, she got the news that they were out-bid by $15,000. Larry would be home as soon as he fixed a few bugs in his new project.

* *

After they lost the bid, Abby quit her job at KiddyCare and started volunteering at the Community Center. She was helping folks, primarily senior citizens who were very ill, to get their affairs in order and get ready to go to the Gateway Transition Center. Her experience with her father helped her in many ways, but when the question came up about what happens at the Center, she couldn't support them. No one knew; it was kept secret by the government. The Centers were located in remote areas, away from towns and away from the protest groups who disagreed with the government's method of population control. The prevalent rumor among the volunteers was that the whole process only took a few days, maybe a week at most and that "guests" was treated very well and, if possible, granted a last wish.

Although they never discussed it, Larry stopped bidding for BEDs on e-Auction. He suggested they take part of the bid money and travel, cruise, and see some glaciers before they all melted or fly to Africa to visit one of the remaining animal preserves. He was surfing travel sites at work, although Abby didn't understand why management claimed he would approve.

There were no more lunches with Barbara; Abby hated her sister. How could she be so selfish? Not hearing the outcome of her mother's "thinking about it," she drove to her mother's house and confronted her one morning.

"Mom, you know I want a baby. Barbara already has Anna. Why would you give your BED to her? It wouldn't be fair — I'm your daughter too."

"I'm not dead yet, and you two are fighting over me. Maybe I should donate my BED to the national lottery. Look, you and Larry have a good life; so does Barbara. I love you, but I wouldn't have children if I had it to do over. It's too late for Barbara, but you don't have to have babies. It's not a good world anymore. "

It was no use. Her mother turned away from Abby and started folding laundry.

"OK, mom, we'll discuss this some other time. I'm sorry. I love you."

Weeks passed, and soon it would be Thanksgiving, and the extended family would be together — an event that started after her dad died. Abby was not looking forward to it. She couldn't think of a single reason to give thanks for anything.

* *

The Gilbert house is large, a carryover from when energy was abundant and cheap. Abby entered the front door behind Larry, carrying the marshmallow-topped sweet potatoes, their contribution to the feast. The smell of roasted turkey brought back memories of their first Thanksgiving here when she and Larry were dating. For her, the rooms still echoed with plans they had made to marry and have a family.

The large table was covered with food, bowls of mashed potatoes, gravy, sage and cinnamon stuffing, Abby's sweet potatoes, and in the center, an enormous turkey artfully carved by Larry's dad.

After a prayer, the bowls were passed around the circle. Abby took tiny portions; she had little appetite. The labor of days of cooking was consumed in minutes, and the woman waited while the men attacked a smaller, second plate of food until forks rattled onto the plates signaling defeat.

Larry's dad rose.

"Let's help the woman clear the table so we can have dessert and coffee."

A synchronized "groan" filled the room.

" But first, I'd like us to go around the room, and each of us tells what they're grateful for. We have so much."

Anna shouted: "Me, I want to be first."

"I'm grateful for my mom and dad, Grandma and Grandpa Gilbert, and my best friend Carolyn at school. And I am grateful that I'm going to have a …."

Barbara stopped abruptly: "Thank you, Anna; now let's hear from Grandma and Grandpa."

Larry's dad was smiling. "I'm grateful that we can all be here together." And looking at Larry, he said: "Your mother and I are grateful for our health. I have little arthritis, but my doctor said I could live to be 100. We have a good life, and I want to do this again next year and the next, God willing."

Mom Gilbert nodded and gestured to Larry. His mind was blank, but he had to say something.

"You're hearing it for the first time: I've been promoted, and I'm getting an office with a door. You're looking at a new software manager and one grateful person."

Abby stared at Larry.

Barbara was next.

"I have much to be thankful for, my husband and little Anna. And I'm blessed to have such a wonderful mother. Thanks, mom. I will never forget this Thanksgiving."

Barbara's husband quickly added: "she said it all."

Abby's mother looked at her. "Abby, I'm so grateful you and Larry are happy. I was worried for a while, but I know you will be OK." She turned to Barbara. "You have a beautiful family, and you're such a wonderful mother. I've lived a long life. And now, I'm at peace."

Abby looked around the table. She saw that everyone was looking at her, expecting some expression to make the day complete and excellent. Larry raised his index finger and nodded. It was her turn.

"I'm grateful I haven't been sterilized and can still have a baby."

"Abby..." Larry's mouth hung wide.

The room was silent and spinning; she didn't know what to say next.

"I'm not feeling well. I have to go. Larry, I'll be at home; you stay."

"OK, Abby, but you get some rest. I'll get dad to drive me home after the cleanup."

Abby ran to the car. But she didn't head for home; she drove around. The streets were empty primarily — all those families sitting at tables being grateful. After a while, without thinking, she started going out of town. After passing the large homes with big yards, she entered the country and noticed that there were still a few farms and open spaces left. It was beautiful. Although past their autumn peak, the leaves magically colored the countryside, reminding her of childhood trips to see the leaves. She felt something being released inside of her. She knew what to do.

She pulled off the road and stopped the car at the guardhouse. The young man who had caught Thanksgiving duty raised his eyebrows in surprise.

"Hello. You going in?"

"Yes."

"What about your car? I mean, who's going to drive it home?"

Abby lied: "I've arranged for someone to pick it up."

"OK, but you only have 24 hours to have the car removed. Drive to the reception building. It's about one mile."

Abby thought the high fence and the long driveway must be to keep protesters away. It was deserted; maybe they took the day off. She stopped the car in a parking lot near a large building. At first, it looked like a hotel, but she noticed it had no genuine windows. There were faux windows with flower boxes and window ledges but no glass. She guessed it was three or four stories high; it was hard to tell. The massive industrial chimney slightly behind the building threw her off.

The large doors opened, then closed behind her. It was a lobby with dimly lit dark mahogany paneling and a reception desk under a tasteful sign: "Gateway Transition Reception."

"Hello, I'm Abby Gilbert; I'm here to ...."

"Yes, of course. Please take a seat over there, and I'll have a TS guide you in."

"TS?"

"Transition Specialist."

A middle-aged woman in a finely tailored business suit greeted Abby with a smile. His name tag read: "Judith."

"Welcome, let's see, you're Abby. Well, you're making a good decision. Let's go back to my office and fill out some forms. How is the weather out there? Did you enjoy your drive?"

Judith's office carried the same lobby theme: more dark paneling and warm lighting. Her desk was empty except for a vase of fresh fall flowers, and on the side, a picture frame with two small smiling children facing Abby. She saw Abby staring at the children.

"My grandchildren. Aren't they lovely?"

Abby's heart twisted.

Abby, please fill out these forms. You can fill in the particulars later, but first, I need to ask a few key questions.

"Who gets your BED document?"

Abby thought for a moment and then responded.

"Jennifer. Jennifer Collins. She's my cousin. She's getting married in a few weeks. Maybe we can find her address in the phone book."

"We can do that later. Here is the fun part: "What is your last wish?"

The rumors were true. After some thought, she put her hand on her stomach and replied softly:

"I have none; I have everything I want."

After completing the paperwork, Judith offered Abby a Thanksgiving dinner, which she refused, then guided her to her room. On the way, she saw another Gateway resident — an older man in a wheelchair, being pushed by a tall blond woman in a low-cut dress, high heels, and a beauty mark. The woman bent over and kissed his cheek.

CHAPTER 97

BOOK EXCERPT: "MADE IN AMERICA" CHAPTER ONE

The US recession of 2008 was declared to be over, but the economy of Pittsburgh, Pennsylvania, never recovered. The closing of the steel mills in the early eighties started their economic slide, and now the race for global economic dominance has been decided—China has won. It's now 2015, and a large Chinese auto company, wanting to establish a US presence and ignoring the affront to the people of Pittsburgh, has built an auto factory along the Monongahela river where the steel mills were once located. The Chinese cars would be made in America.

Young Cole Edwards wanted to follow in his father's footsteps and become an engineer, but his father, finding no engineering job, worked as a foreman in a Chinese auto parts factory. Should Cole follow his father into the factory or go to Carnegie Mellon University and pursue his dream? Influenced by his father, Cole, believes China's success is unfair and holds them to blame for his family's decline.

Cole's anger toward the Chinese is challenged when he begins dating the "enemy," Qiang Li, the daughter of the auto plant manager. Getting permission to date her starts with a small lie; soon, his whole family lies, each for their reason. Everything Cole believes about the Chinese people, how to love, and how to make your way in this new-world economy is proven wrong.

THE IDIOT

"Cole, you're a fucking idiot. No, I take it back; you're just an ordinary idiot. I know you're not getting any from Alejandra."

Too fast and without thinking, Cole blurted, "I'm gettin' a lot." He knew his best friend, Brent, wouldn't believe him. Alejandra was his girlfriend, and they had gone pretty far but weren't getting any. Best friends know these things, and he and Brent shared everything, but now he wanted no part of Cole's bellyaching about what to do with his life.

Brent ignored Cole and continued working on a joint, first compacting it, then licking the paper, compressing it again, and finally twisting it. It looked like a white twig, but it smoked pretty well. It was a technique Brett said he learned from two black guys from the Hill District. They called it a "ghetto wrap." He lit the joint with the barbecue lighter from the nearby Weber, tilting his head sideways to avoid singeing his hair, and taking a deep drag, handed it to Cole.

With smoke still in his lungs, his voice thin and strained, almost hissing, he turned to Cole. "I'm sick of hearing about your problem. If you want to be a God-damned engineer, then do it. I think you're crazy. Look at your dad; for Christ's sake, he's got an engineering degree, and he's working in a factory. Do you think there are any engineering jobs left in Pittsburgh?"

Cole didn't answer. He was looking around, worried about their neighbors, wondering if someone was looking out a window at the two boys on the back porch of their family home. It had been his grandfather's and now his dad's inheritance. Grandfather had been a successful software engineer who had spent some time in Silicon Valley before moving back to marry his grandmother and build this house in the affluent community of Mount Lebanon. Cole's family had been pretending for years that they had the income to live in the big house, hiding that his mother was an admin at Carnegie Mellon University and his father was a factory worker. The lack of home repairs was beginning to show, there were two beat-up cars hidden in the garage, and now, pot smoking by the young Edward's boy would signal their lower class status.

"Fuck you." He paused for emphasis. "You have it made. Your father will give you a job at Alcoa—some cushy desk job—you'll marry a blond nympho and have two kids and a dog."

"So?"

"I don't know; I want to be an engineer and stay here in the Burg. What's wrong with that? Maybe I'll marry Alejandra and finally be a fucking idiot."

They both laughed.

"Cole, you bastard, you're dragging me into the same old conversation; I'm not going there. Next, you'll be bitchin' how the Chinese are taking over the town. That's how your dad got a job, right? In the Chinese car plant?"

"Keep my dad out of this. He's just doing what he can. It's not his fault."

"Yea, and you're going to do what you can. You might as well march down there after graduation and join your dad. Why waste your time in four years of college?"

Cole pondered Brent's harsh words. His friend could be cruel sometimes, but they had always been there for each other. And in the back of his mind, he knew Brent was right. Did his dad try to get an engineering job, or was something wrong, something flawed about him? Recently, the long-dormant issue about his father's employment resurfaced. During dinner arguments, his mom suggested he wasn't trying. His father absorbed her attack for a while and stormed off to his basement workshop. Cole didn't want to marry Alejandra and spend the rest of his life having the same conversation with her. He wanted it to be decided now, so he could let go of his fear and enjoy the rest of his senior year. Probably Alejandra knew something was wrong in Edward's household, and that's why she was holding back. She was from a Mexican-American family, and Cole would appear to be a good catch—a rich white boy living in a big house in Mount Lebanon, collegebound to a good life. Maybe she sensed his fears; perhaps she knew he didn't love her; he never said he did, even when touching her. Why would I marry her? These feelings were swirling around in his head, and he faced Brent with a blank, speechless expression.

"Cole, ... hello! He waved his arms in front of Cole's face. Look, I'm sorry; I didn't mean all that stuff. Why not go to college and decide all that shit later. For God's sake, your mom works there. All you need is lunch money." He paused, but Cole was still lost in thought. "Here, take a drag on this," carefully handing him the roach in a tiny clip.

With some difficulty, Cole took a puff, released the clip, and let the butt fall to the deck. He got on his knees, poked it out with stabbing blows from his fingers, and carefully scraped the remains between the deck boards. When he stood up, he felt light-headed and dizzy. He struggled to answer his friend. "You're right... I need to go to college, ... have some fun. I'm not like my dad. All this stuff can wait." He paused and, feeling less dizzy, shifted the conversation to the present.

"About that lunch money, I could get a job in the summer. The auto plant is having a Job Faire at school. We could work together, you know, make a few cars, maybe take them around town for a test drive."

"Why would they want to hire kids like us when Pittsburgh has so many unemployed men?

"Because we're cheap. Anyway, that's what my dad says."

"Cheap, yeah, those Chinese bastards want to pay us coolie wages? I don't know if I want to work in some chink factory."

"Brent, it's just for the summer."

He was not convinced, Cole knew that, but it was still a long time until summer. He would come around.

As they moved toward the patio door, Brent put his hand on Cole's shoulder and swung him around.

"Hey, exactly what are you getting from Alejandra? A little tit?"

"Lots."

www.ingramcontent.com/pod-product-compliance
Lightning Source LLC
Chambersburg PA
CBHW070543010526
44118CB00012B/1202